DIY Hydroponics

System Builders Guide

DIY Hydroponics
System Builders Guide
Third Edition

John P. Hennessy

DiyHydroponics.com

Legal Disclaimers

All contents copyright © 2009 Diy Hydroponics. All rights reserved. No part of this document or accompanying files may be reproduced or transmitted in any form, electronic or otherwise, by any means without the prior written permission of the publisher.

This ebook is presented to you for informational purposes only and is not a substitution for any professional advice. The contents herein are based on the views and opinions of the author and all associated contributors.

While every effort has been made by the author and all associated contributors to present accurate and up to date information within this document, it is apparent technologies rapidly change. Therefore, the author and all associated contributors reserve the right to update the contents and information provided herein as these changes progress. The author and or all associated contributors take no responsibility for any errors or omissions if such discrepancies exist within this document.

The author and all other contributors accept no responsibility for any consequential actions taken, whether monetary, legal, or otherwise, by any and all readers of the materials provided. It is the reader's sole responsibility to seek professional advice before taking any action on their part.

Readers results will vary based on their skill level and individual perception of the contents herein, and thusly no guarantees, monetarily or otherwise, can be made accurately. Therefore, no guarantees are made.

ISBN: 9781468072723

DIY Hydroponics System Builders Guide

Table of Contents

Introduction 5

Chapter 1: Ebb & Flow Systems 6

Chapter 2: Top Feed Systems 18

Chapter 3: NFT Systems 27

Chapter 4: MPT Tray Systems 45

Hydroponic Resources 58

Glossary 59

Introduction

Using This Guide

The plans in this guide provide instructions for building your own hydroponics garden system. In most cases, it is only necessary to obtain the tools and materials, and then to follow the pictures to assemble the systems. Most of the required materials can be purchased at your local home or builder supply store such as Home Depot or Lowe's. Some other good sources for materials include hardware stores, and irrigation, farm, and industrial supply stores. For Rubber-maid type totes and containers try Target, K-mart, Wal-Mart, etc. You can also purchase your parts and supplies from online hydroponics and garden suppliers.

When using this manual, it is not necessary to follow each step and measurements precisely. Use these instructions as a guide. Be creative and flexible; adjust the plans to create your own custom system. For example, you may find a container that you believe would make a good reservoir or growing tray, but the size is not exactly the same as in the plans. Simply adjust the PVC pipes used to hold the tray to fit your container. Once you understand the basic principles, you should be able to modify and create many variations of the systems in this guide.

If you are new to hydroponics, I recommend that you start with the small ebb & flow system. It is very easy to build and works both indoors and outdoors. Adjusting the flood cycle and controlling the PH level will help you get a feel for hydroponic gardening and prepare you to move on to a larger system.

Good luck and grow have fun!

John P. Hennessy

DiyHydroponics.com

Chapter 1 - Ebb & Flow Systems

Introduction:

Ebb & Flow Hydroponic Systems, (also known as the "Flood and Drain") are easy to build and simple to operate. A small system can be assembled in less than one hour with just a few simple parts. Ebb & Flow Systems are commonly used to grow: peppers, herbs, lettuces, potted flowers, and other plants.

How it Works:

A pump is connected to a timer, which is set to turn on and flood the growing tray at set intervals. When the timer comes on, the growing tray fills up until the water level reaches the overflow tube. The overflow tube sets the water level in the growing tray. When the timer turns the pump off, the remainder of the water will drain out of the growing tray and back to the reservoir through the fill inlet. The timer is set to run flood cycles throughout the day. A complete cycle usually runs from 15 to 30 minutes and is repeated every two to four hours. The timer is usually set to leave the pump off at night.

Planting:

Use an inert medium that retains some moisture in order to provide a buffer between flood cycles. Plant in pots or fill the entire grow tray with media. Some common hydroponics mediums include: Perlite, Coca fiber, pea gravel, and Lecastone (expanded clay pebbles).

Ebb & Flow Building Notes:

The growing tray is a key component of the Ebb & Flow System. Choose a plastic tray that is large enough to hold your pots. It should be around 3 to 6 inches deep and flat-bottomed for good drainage. The tray should also be strong enough to hold the pots, media, and water when flooded. Some tray suggestions are: a kitty litter box, dishpan, cement/mortar mixing tray, a Rubber-Maid, or other plastic storage container. The reservoir should be large enough to hold 3 times the amount of water required to flood the growing tray. The fill and drain fittings can be purchased at any Hydroponics supplier, or you can build your own DIY fittings from common PVC pipe parts.

Example #1: Ebb & Flow System Using a Kitty Litter Tray

Required Materials:

- 1 – plastic tray to use as the growing tray (Rubber-maid, kitty litter, dish pan, etc)
- 1 – plastic container to use as a reservoir
- 1 – fill and overflow drain fittings (buy or build these)
- 1 – timer (household electric timer with no less than 30 min intervals)
- 1 – small fountain pump (it must pump to the height of the bottom of the growing tray)
- 2 – feet of ½ inch ID flexible tubing to connect pump to fill fitting (do not use *clear* tubing)
- 2 to 6 pots and enough media to fill them (any small pots 3 to 10 inches with drain holes)

Required Tools: 1 inch drill or a razor knife to cut the holes in the tray and reservoir top.

DIY Hydroponics System Builders Guide

Step 1: Drill or cut two 1 inch holes in the bottom of the growing tray as shown. Drill the two holes ½ to 1 inch apart from each other. Be sure to drill gently, it is easy to crack the bottom of some weaker trays. If you do not have a drill, you can use a sharp razor knife to carefully cut the holes.

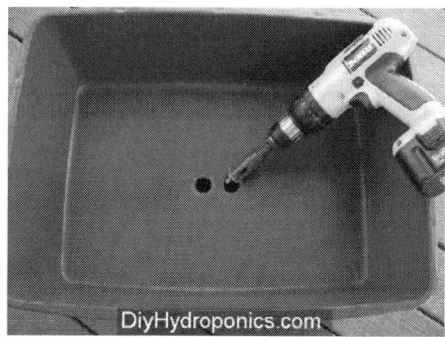

Step 2: Install the Ebb & Flow fittings. Push the fittings through the holes in the top of the tray and secure underneath the tray with the female threaded couplers. The rubber washer should go on the topside for the overflow and on the underside for the fill fitting. (See pictures below)

Note: You will need to adjust the overflow drain according to the height of your pots. The GH fittings included with our kits are preset for 2 inches. You may change the fill depth by using a longer piece of ¾ inch PVC pipe on the overflow drain. The idea is to fill the tray to 1 to 2 inches below the top of your pots. Keeping the tops of the pots dry will reduce algae growth.

(*Pictures of Ebb & Flow fittings installed in tray*)

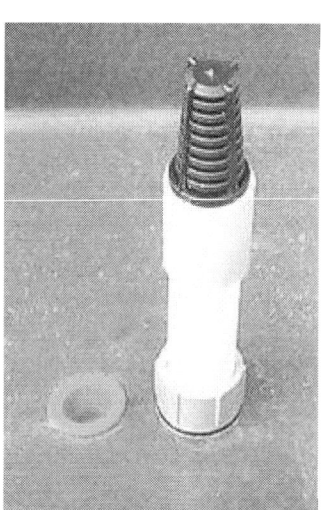

Note: Instructions for building DIY fittings are given in Ebb & Flow example #2 and step #5.

Step 3: Drill or cut one 3 to 4 inch hole or two 1 inch holes in the top of the reservoir. Orientate the holes so that when the growing tray is set on top, the fill and drain fittings will pass through the holes.

(Fittings and tubing pass through this hole in the reservoir top.)

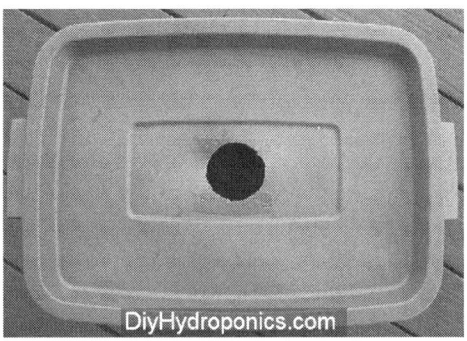

Step 4: Place the pump in the reservoir and connect to the fill fitting with a piece of 1/2inch ID flexible tubing. Leave the tubing long enough so that you will be able to lift the tray off the reservoir to service the pump. Be careful not to make any sharp bends in the tubing, use an elbow if necessary. Set the growing tray on top of the reservoir, fill with water, and test the pump and drain. Adjust the fill level in the tray by changing the height of the overflow drain. Finally place the planted pots in the tray, add nutrients, and set the timer.

(The completed, ready to plant, Ebb & Flow System)

DIY Hydroponics System Builders Guide

Example #2: Ebb & Flow Using a Mortar Mixing Tray

Required Materials:

- 1 – 28 by 20 cement/mortar mixing tray (from Home Depot)
- 1 – fill and drain fittings (GH fitting or DIY version from PVC parts)
- 1 – 6 inch piece of ¾ inch PVC pipe (used to route the drain back to the reservoir)
- 1 – 12 to 18 gallon reservoir (Any plastic container less than 17" tall will fit under stand)
- 1 – cycle timer (with 15 to 30 minute intervals)
- 1 – small submersible pump
- 1 – ½" flexible tubing 18" to 24" long (connects pump to growing tray)
- 4 – zip ties or some wire (used to hold growing tray onto stand)

Parts List for growing tray stand: (¾ inch PVC pipe and connectors or use 1 inch for a stronger stand)

- 2 – 18 inch (for cross members, sets the stand depth)
- 2 – 26 ¼ inch (front & back rails)
- 4 – 22 inch (legs)
- 8 – elbows (connects it all together)

Step #1: Assemble the Growing Tray Stand

a. Use four elbows, four 22"pipes, and two 18"pipes to build the leg assemblies shown in figure #1.
b. Use four elbows and two 26 ¼ inch pipes to build the top rails in figure #2.
c. Connect the top rails to the leg assemblies to complete the stand as shown in figure #3.

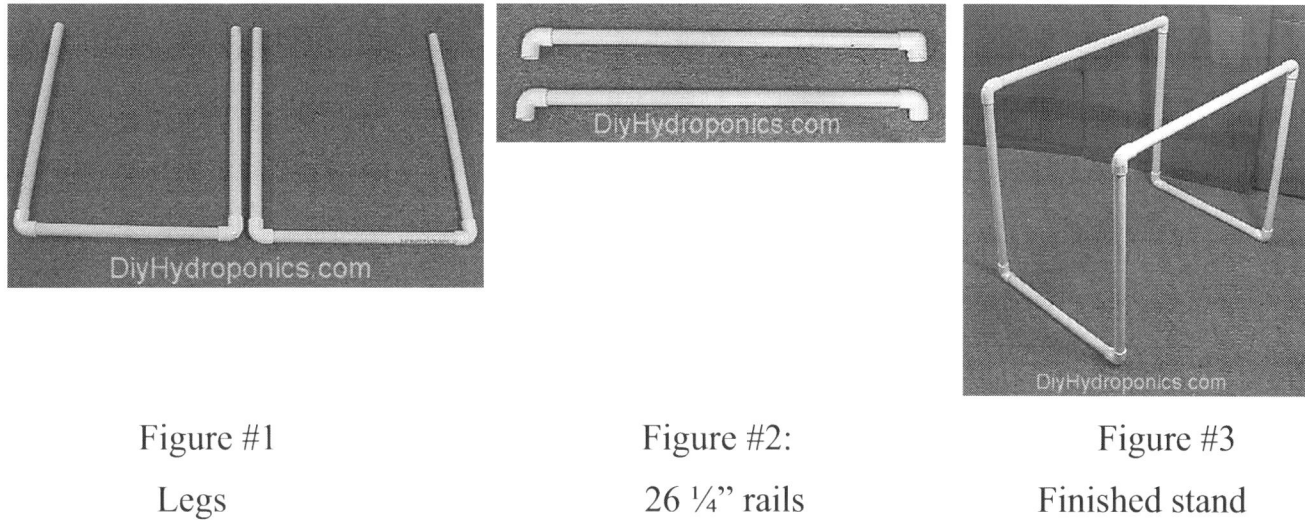

Figure #1	Figure #2:	Figure #3
Legs	26 ¼" rails	Finished stand

The assembly of the growing tray stand is now complete.

Note: If you desire to build the optional light stand, please continue to Step #2. If you *do not* wish to build the light stand please skip to *Step #3*.

Step #2: Building the Optional Light Stand

You will use the parts listed below, to construct the light stand shown in figure #8

Parts for the optional light stand include:

- 4 – 28 inch pipes (light stand posts)
- 4 – 8 ¼ inch pipes
- 2 – 18 inch pipes
- 4 – elbows
- 10 – tees
- 1 – 26 ¼ inch pipe

DIY Hydroponics System Builders Guide

Follow steps 2A and 2B to modify the bottom stand that you built in Step #1.

Step 2A: To enable the growing tray stand to accommodate the optional light stand, you must replace the 4 upper elbows in figures #4, with 4 tee's as shown in figure #5

Step 2B: Build the two assemblies in figure #6. Attach four 28 inch legs as shown in figure #7. Connect the two assemblies together with one 26 ¼ inch pipe as shown below in figure #8. Put the light stand on top of the growing tray stand as shown below in figure #9.

Figure #4

4 elbows on top rails

Figure #5

Modified stand with 4 tee's

Figure #6

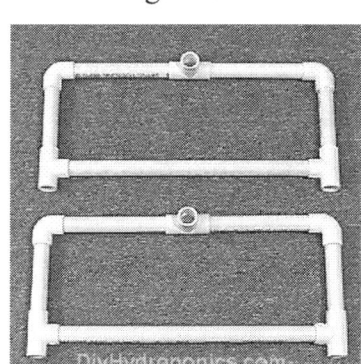

Figure #7

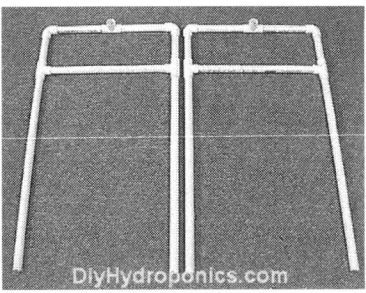

Figure #8

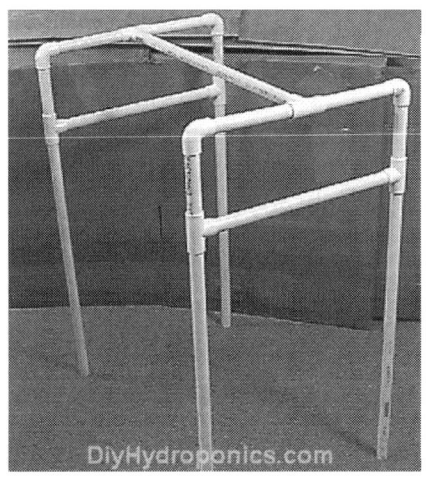

Figure #9

Step #3: Attach the Growing Tray to the Stand

Drill four ¼ inch holes in the long sides of the growing tray. Drill the holes approximately 7 inches from the end of the tray and 1 inch down inside the tray. Use four zip ties or pieces of wire to securely attach the growing tray to the stand.

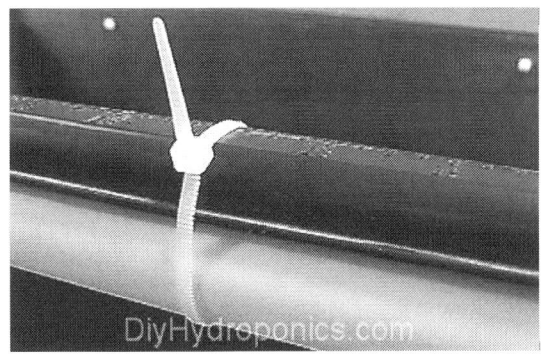 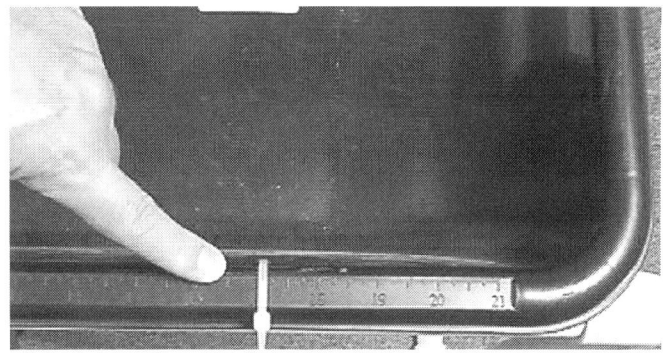

Step #4: Install the Ebb & Flow Fittings

a. Drill or cut two 1 inch holes in the bottom of the grow tray. Drill the two holes ½ to 1 inch apart from each other. Drill gently, it is easy to crack the bottom of some trays. If you do not have a drill, you can use a sharp razor knife to carefully cut the holes.

b. Install the Ebb & Flow fittings as shown. Push the fittings through the holes in the top of the tray and secure underneath the tray with the female threaded couplers. The rubber washer should go on the topside for the overflow and on the underside for the fill fitting.

Note: You will need to adjust the overflow drain according to the height of your pots. The GH fittings included with our kits are preset for 2 inches. You may change the fill depth by using a longer piece of ¾ inch PVC pipe on the overflow drain. The idea is to fill the tray to 1 to 2 inches below the top of your pots. Keeping the tops of the pots dry will reduce algae growth.

(Pictures of Ebb & Flow fittings installed in tray)

 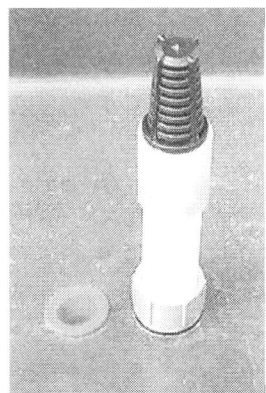 

DIY Hydroponics System Builders Guide

Step #5: Building the DIY Ebb & Flow Fittings from PVC Parts

Note: *Skip this step if you purchased ebb & flow fittings.*

Required Materials:

- 2 – ¾ inch male threaded couplers (one end threaded male)
- 1 – ¾ inch double female threaded coupler (threaded female on both ends)
- 1 – ¾ inch single female threaded coupler (threaded female on one end)
- 2 – ¾ inch ID rubber washers
- 1 – 6 inch piece of ¾ inch PVC Pipe (for bottom side of overflow drain)
- 1 – 2 to 4 inch piece of ¾ inch PVC Pipe (For top side of overflow drain, adjust length for your pots)
- 1 – PVC Adapter with male threads on one end and ½ hose barb on the other

a. Use a hack saw to cut off one of the male threaded couplers just above the threads and nut. See the pen pointing to the spot to cut the fitting (Figure #1). This will become the fill fitting.

b. Push the new fill fitting (see Figure #2 on left) through one of the holes in the topside of the tray and secure it underneath the tray with a rubber washer and a double sided female threaded coupler.

c. Screw the ¾ inch male threaded to ½ inch hose barb adapter into the double female threaded coupler.

   (I often use a little Teflon tape on all the male threads to create a better seal.)

d. Push the other male threaded coupler through the other hole in the topside of the tray. Secure it underneath with a rubber washer and the single female threaded coupler. This is the overflow drain.

e. Connect a 2 to 4 inch piece of ¾ inch pipe to the top of the drain tube. The length of this pipe will set the water level in the tray. Change the length of this pipe so that the flood level in the tray will be about 1 to 2 inches below the top of your pots. (See Figure #3)

f. Connect an approximately 6 inch long piece of ¾ inch PVC pipe to the bottom of the overflow drain fitting. Change the length of this pipe, so that it will protrude a couple inches through the top of your reservoir. This completes the overflow drain assembly. (See Figure #4)

DiyHydroponics.com

Figures: 1-4

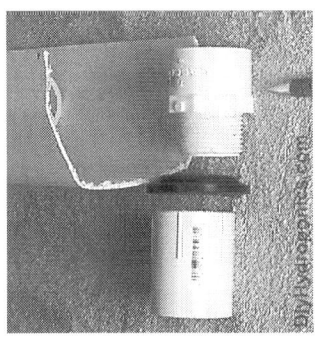

Figure #1

Pen is pointing to spot to be cut on fill fitting

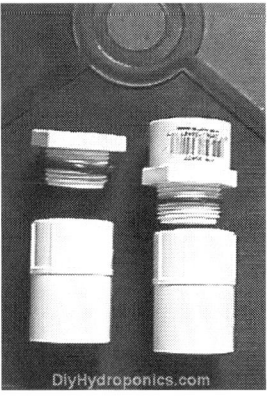

Figure #2

Notice that the fill on the left is now cut. Do not cut the overflow drain

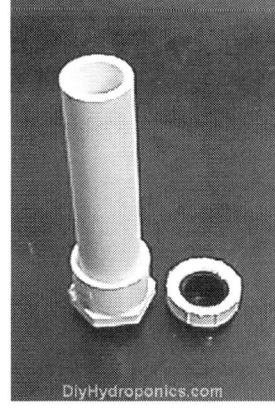

Figure #3

Top side overflow drain is on the left and the fill is on the right

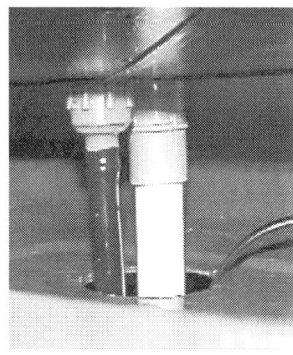

Figure #4

Fittings protruding through the hole in the reservoir lid.

Step #6: Drill or cut one 3 to 4 inch hole or two 1 inch holes in the top, of the reservoir. (See Step #5, Figure 4: your fill and drain fittings will pass through this hole.)

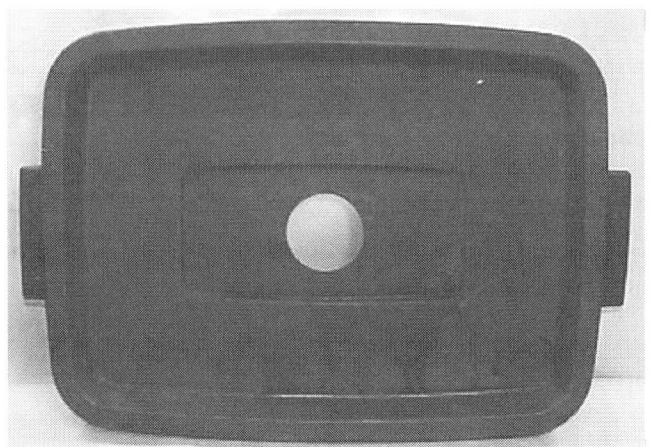

Step #7: Place the pump into the reservoir and attach the ½ inch ID flexible fill line from the pump to the fill connector on the growing tray. Fill with water, plug in the timer and pump, and test the system. You have completed the Ebb & Flow System.

DIY Hydroponics System Builders Guide

Pictures of completed system:

Ebb & Flow Building and Operating Tips:

The PVC Stand
Press the PVC parts together with a twist and then pound them tight together. For a stronger stand, you can use 1 inch PVC or glue the parts with PVC glue. The height of the bottom stand and top light stand can easily by adjusting the length of the vertical PVC pipes.

Alternative Growing Trays
For our example system, we used a 28 x 20 x 6 inch mortar-mixing tray from Home Depot. They are used to mix concrete, dry wall, mud and plaster. Another good choice is a restaurant bus tray. Bus trays are smaller but stronger than the mortar mixing trays. Any tray that you use should be made of plastic or wood that has been sealed and covered with plastic. Adjust the length and width of the stand to fit your tray.

Testing and Adjusting your Ebb & Flow System
Fill the reservoir with water. Plug in the pump and make sure the growing tray fills and drains out the overflow. Check for leaks in the reservoir, growing tray, and around the plumbing fittings. If anything leaks, tighten and/or seal with waterproof silicon glue. Now turn off the pump and make sure the growing tray drains out as completely as possible.

Cleaning your System
Between crops, remove the debris from the growing tray, pots, and reservoir. Flush everything with a water and bleach solution. Rinse and wipe dry.

Cycle Times
Ebb and flow cycles will vary depending on the type of plants, medium used, and environmental conditions. A good starting point is to flood the growing tray from 15 to 30 minutes every 2 to 6 daylight hours, with a rest period at night. A good trial and error method to determine the optimal cycle is to decrease the time between flooding until the plants show signs of distress by slightly wilting. Then increase the cycle intervals until there is no sign of wilting. This should provide a nearly optimal flood cycle. Plants may also require longer or more frequent flooding cycles depending on the time of year and stage of growth.

Nutrient Temperature
Ideally, a nutrient temperature of 18 to 22°C should be maintained for optimum growth. However this temperature may change depending on the crop and location of the system. Shield your reservoir from the sun or use insulation to keep the nutrient cool. If your nutrient is too cold, insulate the reservoir tank or use a fish tank heater or heating pad to warm the nutrient.

Chapter 2: Top Feed Systems

Introduction:

Top feed systems (also known as the "Drip System") are easy to build and simple to operate and maintain. Any type of plant can be grown in a top feed system. Some common commercial crops grown in top feed systems include: tomatoes, peppers, and cucumbers. Many commercial flower growers like to use this systems as well.

How it Works:

A pump is connected to a manifold, which distributes the nutrient solution to each pot through drip lines. The system may run continuously or on a timer. The flow can also be controlled with valves or regulated drippers. The secret to a well performing top feed system is to keep the media moist, but not over soaked. If your media is getting too wet, use a control valve to regulate the flow of nutrients to the plants.

Planting:

One or two plants are planted in each pot. Plants are planted in a media such as perlite or coca fiber. For large plants, pots are usually spaced 16 or more inches apart. Vine crops, like tomatoes and cucumbers, will need a trellis or cable with hanging twine to support the climbing vines.

Note: *A large plant, such as tomatoes, can consume up to 1 gallon of water each day. Use a large reservoir or a float valve and a fresh water connection to keep the reservoir full.*

Note: *Drip lines can become clogged. For a safe-guard, run two lines to each pot, or use a filter.*

Example #1: Small Top Feed System

Use this modification to convert an Ebb & Flow System into a Top Feed System.

Required Materials:

- 1 – drip manifold with 6 outlets
- 1 – ½ inch male to ½ inch hose bib adapter
- 6 – ¼ inch drip lines and stakes
- 1 – 6 inch piece of ¾ inch PVC pipe (used to raise the drip manifold)

For conversion, follow these 3 steps.

1. Replace the short overflow PVC drainpipe with a 6 inch long piece of PVC pipe and route the ½ tubing from the pump through this pipe as shown.

2. Connect the drip manifold to the flexible fill line using the PVC to hose barb adapter.

3. Run drip lines from the drip manifold to the pots and hold in place with the drip stakes.

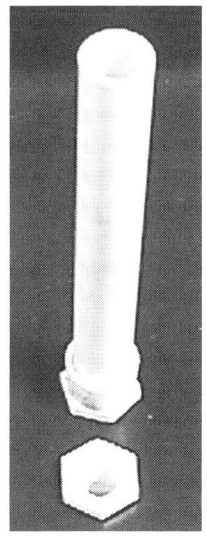

Your completed ebb and flow to drip conversion.

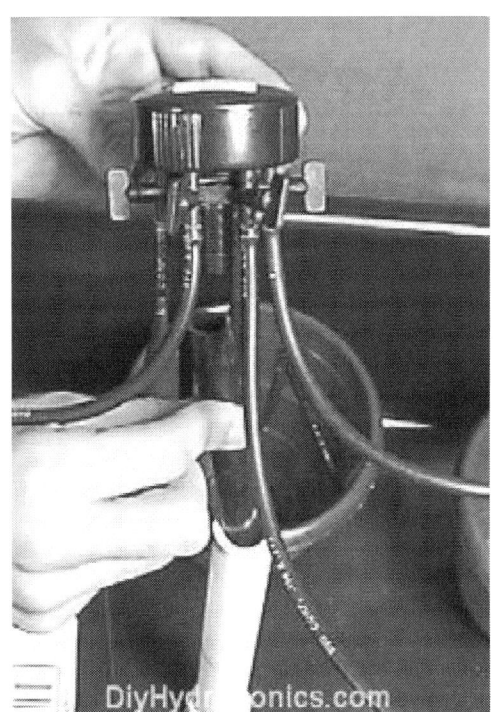

Example #2: Small 4 Bucket Elevated Bato System

Introduction:

Bato Buckets, also known as "Dutch Pots" are commonly used for growing tomatoes, cucumbers, Peppers and other plants. Systems are simple to setup and can be expanded from 1 to 100's of pots.

Planting:

Bato Buckets use an inert media for planting. Perlite is the most common along with a mix of perlite and some other media such vermiculite or coca fiber. Other media include Lecastone (expanded clay pebbles), pea gravel, volcanic rock, and some types of tree bark.

How They Work:

The Bato buckets are 2.5 gallons in size and are designed with a notched bottom allowing them to sit directly upon a 1 ½ inch PVC drainpipe. Each bucket has two special siphon elbows inside to maintain 1 inch of nutrient in the bottom of the bucket. Excess nutrient flows from the elbows into the drainpipe and back to the reservoir. Bato systems are easily expandable from one to hundreds of buckets. The setup is simple, the Bato's and the drainpipe sit directly on the ground or on an elevated surface or platform. Watering is done through drip lines. You can build your own DIY-style Bato's out of 5 gallon buckets, however you will have a better system if you buy them. Bato Buckets can be purchased along with the elbows from most Hydroponics suppliers for about $7.00 each.

DIY Hydroponics System Builders Guide

Required Parts:

- 4 – Bato buckets with elbows (each bucket will require two elbows)
- 1 – five foot long 1 x 10 or 2 x 12 board (get a treated one if possible)
- 2 – concrete cinder blocks either ½ or full size
- 8 – zip ties or some wire (to hold the drain and fill pipes down on the board and buckets)
- 1 – small submersible pump
- 3 – feet of ½ inch ID flexible tubing (connects fill line to pump)
- 5 – feet of 1 and ½ inch PVC Pipe (for drain pipe)
- 1 – elbow (for drain pipe)
- 1 – cap (for drain pipe)
- 5 – feet of ½ inch PVC pipe
- 1 – elbow with female threads on one end
- 1 – cap for the other end
- 1 – ½ inch male thread to ½ inch hose barb adapter (connects flexible tubing to fill manifold)
- 8 – ¼ inch drip lines 12 to 16 inches long
- 8 – stakes
- 8 – $^{3}/_{8}$ to ¼ inch grommets

Required Tools: Power drill with 1 inch, $^{3}/_{8}$ inch and ¼ inch drill bits, PVC cutter or saw.

Note: *You can have the board and PVC pipes cut by the retailer when you purchase them.*

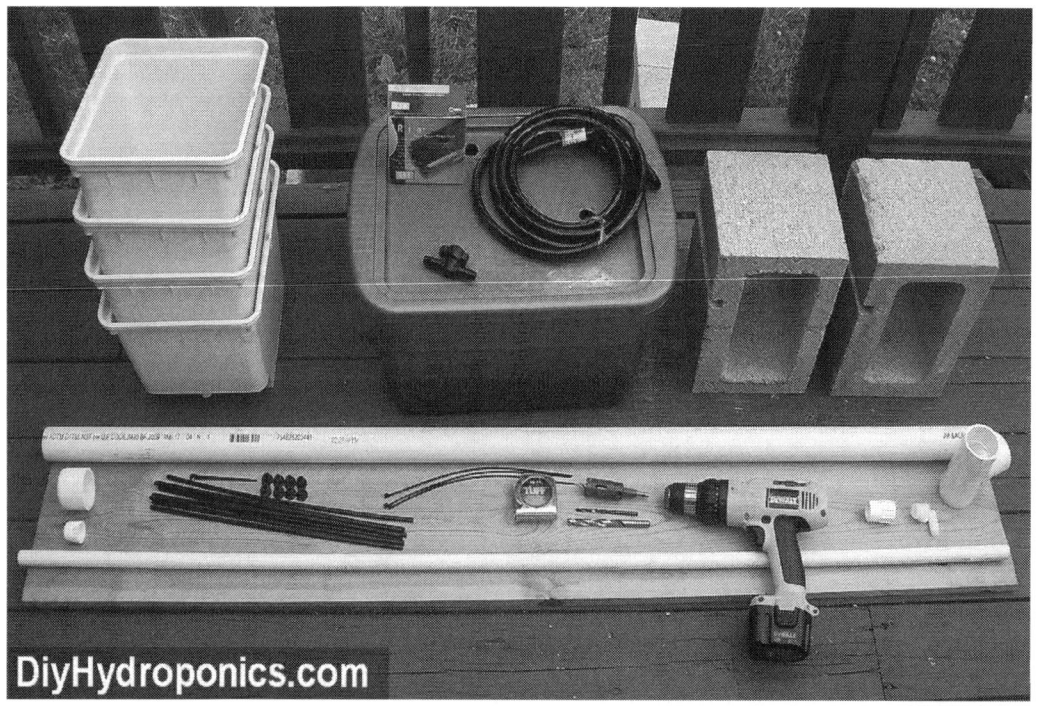

Step #1: Drill the Pipes

a. Drill four 1 inch holes in the 1 ½ inch PVC drain pipe. Drill the first hole 6 inches from one end of the pipe. Drill the next three holes 16 inches apart.

b. Drill eight ³/₈ inch holes in the ½ PVC fill manifold. You will be drilling two holes for each bucket for a total of eight holes. Lay the pipe next to the drilled drainpipe and drill the ³/₈ inch holes about two inches from the center of each drain hole. (See picture below.)

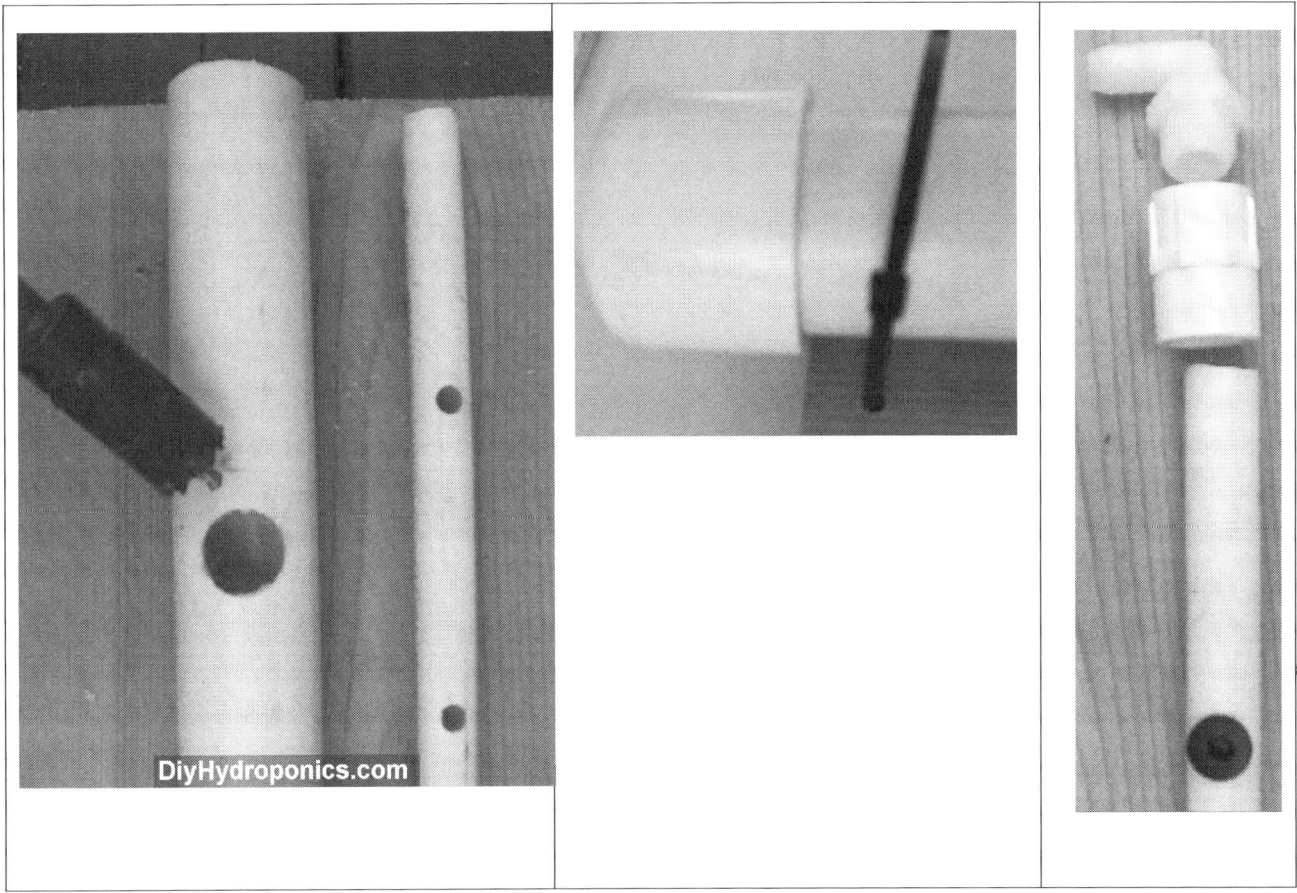

Step #2: Build the Fill and Drain Assemblies

Install a PVC Cap on one end of each PVC pipe. On the other end of the 1 ½ inch drain pipe install an elbow. On the other end of the ½ inch fill pipe install a ½ inch coupler to a female threaded adapter and a ½ inch male thread to ½ inch hose barb adapter. One of these parts should be an elbow that will point downward as pictured below. If you want, you may use some Teflon tape on the male threads to insure a good seal.

DIY Hydroponics System Builders Guide

Step #3: Secure the drain pipe to the board

Place the drainpipe on the board. Line the pipe up on the edge of the board and drill four ¼ inch holes through the board right next to the edge of the pipe. Put zip ties through the holes and secure around the pipe to hold the pipe securely to the board.

Note: *You can substitute ½ inch poly irrigation tubing for the ½ inch PVC fill line assembly. You will need a punch, ¼ inch plug connectors, and an elbow. Get all of these wherever drip irrigation supplies are sold.*

Note: *Most woods will rot if left unprotected from the weather. Cover the board with plastic or use wood sealer, paint, or some other type of wood protection.*

Step #4: Install two elbows inside each bucket and set the buckets on the drain holes.

Step #5: Install the grommets and drip lines

Push a ³⁄₈ inch grommet into each hole in the ½ inch fill pipe. Push a 12 to 16 inch long piece of a ¼ inch drip line into each grommet.

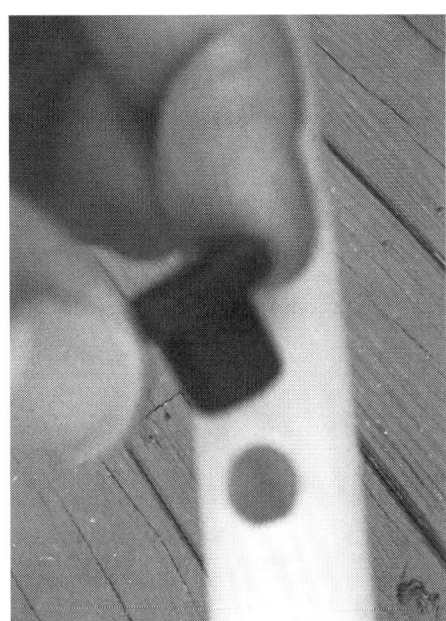 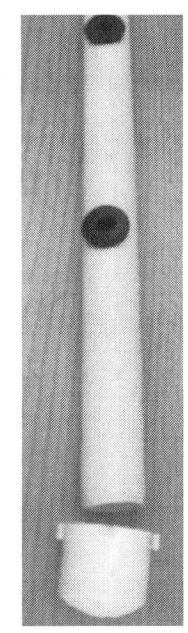 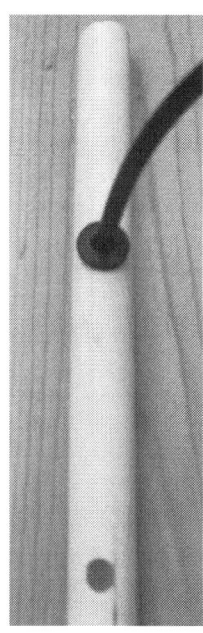

Note: *You can purchase the grommets and 16" drip lines at American Hydroponics.*

Step #6: Secure the fill manifold to the buckets

Drill a ¼ inch hole in the top edge of the buckets, directly above the drain. Using zip ties, secure the ½ inch fill pipe to the top of the buckets. (Figure #6A)

Note: *Alternately, you could also secure the fill manifold to the drainpipe.*

(Figure #6A)

Step # 7: Connect the pump and route the drain into the reservoir

Place the pump in the reservoir and connect to the fill manifold with ½ inch tubing. Use an elbow and a piece of pipe to direct the 1 ½ inch drain pipe to the reservoir.

Pictures of commercial Bato system in greenhouse.

Chapter 3: NFT Systems

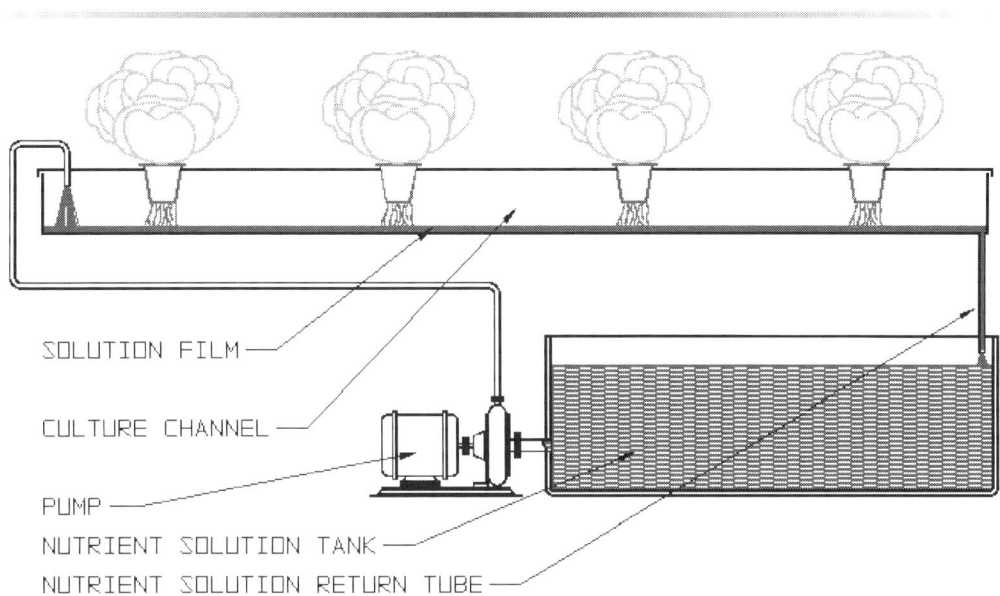

Introduction

NFT (Nutrient film Technique) is the most popular system used by commercial growers for short-term crops. Some commonly grown crops include lettuce, strawberries, and herbs. Tomatoes and other plants are also grown in NFT systems. An advantage of using an NFT system is the plants grow extremely quickly in NFT systems. In fact record growth has been recorded at Miracle Farms. Visit their website for more information. The disadvantages in using NFT, is without any moisture-retaining media, if the pump fails due to electrical or other failure, your plants will quickly die. Careful monitoring or the use of a backup system may be required to prevent the loss of crops.

How it Works:

Plants are placed into flat-bottomed channels (also called gullies) without the use of a media.
A thin film of nutrient flows across the bottom of the channel, continuously feeding the plants. The use of valves and the sloping of the NFT channels enable flow control.

Note: *Although media is never used in a true NFT system, many hobby growers drill out the channel tops for net pots and use a media such as Lecastone (expanded clay pebbles) in the net pots.*

DIY Hydroponics System Builders Guide

Example #1: One and two channel NFT Systems

Materials required:

The PVC Stand   (uses about 50 feet of ¾" sch40 PVC pipe)
- 8 – 16 inch pieces (for cross members, sets the stand depth, use 30" for NFT 24 upgrade)
- 8 – 4 inch pieces (short rails)
- 4 – 38 inch pieces (long rails)
- 4 – 16 inch pieces (legs for bottom stand)
- 4 – 48 inch pieces (legs for top stand)
- 4 – 1 ⁶⁄₈ inch pieces (connects top rails to top tees)
- 8 – PVC elbows
- 16 – PVC tee

The Drain Assembly   (for the crop king channels, use 1 inch PVC pipe for the drain assembly)
- 3 – 1 inch PVC elbows
- 1 – 1 inch PVC tee
- 2 – 6 inch long pipes
- 2 – 2 ½ inch long pipes

The Fill Assembly (Material list for $3/8$ inch clog free manifold)

- 1 – ½ inch male threaded to ½ inch Barb adapter
- 2 – ½ inch PVC caps
- 2 – 3/8 inch threaded barbs
- 2 – 5 ½ inch PVC pipes
- 1 – 64 inches of ½ inch ID flexible tubing and one elbow
- 2 – NFT Channels (4 inch long NFT channels with ends and cover – buy from Crop King)
- 1 – small submersible pump (20 inch lift and a ½ inch discharge)

Note: *Alternate fill manifolds include standard irrigation poly drip line or ½ inch PVC manifold with grommets as discussed in the Bato Bucket Top feed plans*

Preparing to Assemble the 2 or 4 Channel NFT System

Before beginning the project, gather all the PVC fittings and pre-cut all the pipes in the parts list. Be sure to cut the eight ¾ inch cross members PVC pipes to 16 inches long for the 12 plant system or 30 inches long for the 24 plant upgrade, which ever you are building.

Required Tools:

- PVC pipe cutter
- Measuring tape
- Power drill
- Box knife
- Drill bits – $3/16$ inch starter bit and $11/32$ inch bit and a $3/8$ inch tap
- Teflon pipe tape & silicon glue

DIY Hydroponics System Builders Guide

Step #1: Assemble the NFT Channel Support Stand
 A. Use the following PVC parts to build the channel support section as shown.

- 8 – ¾ inch long PVC tees
- 2 – 38 inch long pipes
- 2 – 16 inch long pipes (use 30 inch long pipes for the 24 plant upgrade)
- 4 – 4 inch long pipes

Note: *You will be building two of these if you intend to build the optional light stand.*

Note: *Press the PVC parts together with a twist and then pound them tight together.*

Note: *For a stronger stand use 1inches PVC pipes or glue the parts with PVC glue.*

B. Use the following ¾ inch PVC parts. Build two channel support leg assemblies as shown.

- 4 – PVC elbows
- 6 – 16 inch long pipes (use four 16 inch pipes and two 30 inch pipes for the 24 plant upgrade)

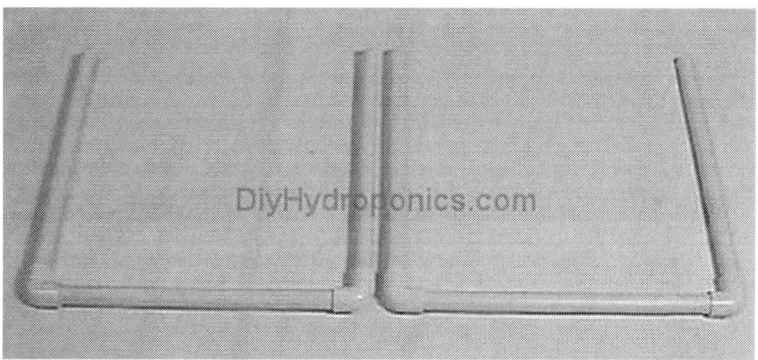

C. Attach the two bottom leg assemblies to the channel support section as shown.

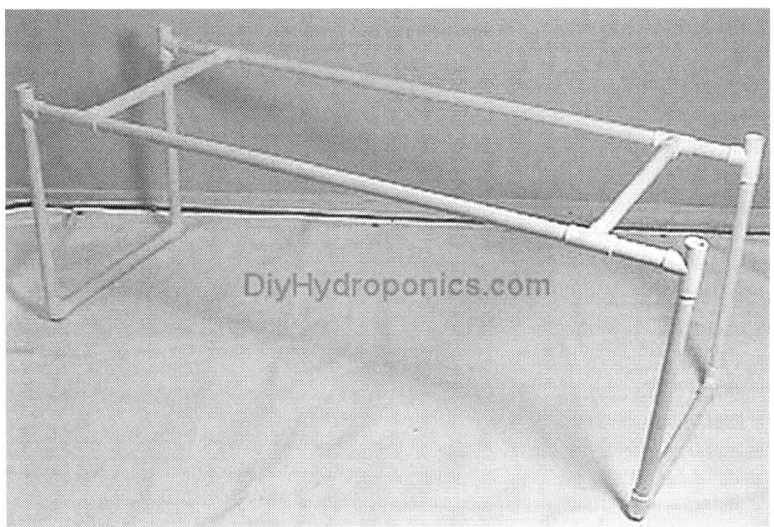

D. Using the parts listed below, build two top rail sections.
- 1 – 16 inch long PVC pipe (30 inch pipe for the NFT 24 upgrade)
- 2 – 1 ⁷/₈ inch long PVC pipes (used on elbows for connecting rail to the top of a tee)
- 2 – PVC elbows

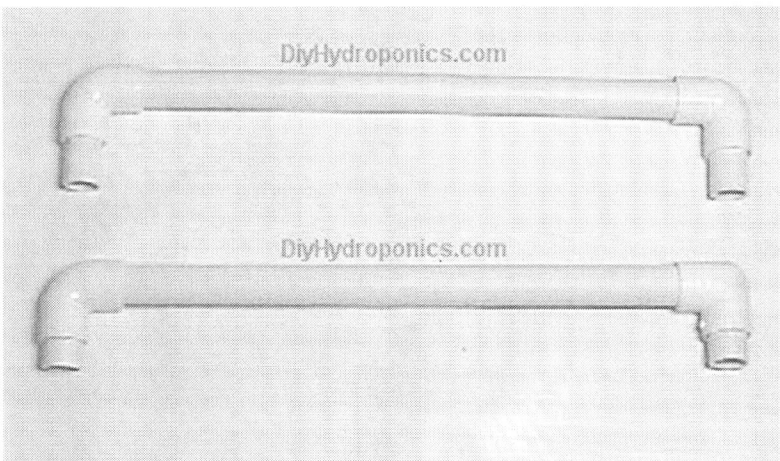

Note: *These two rails will be used on the top light stand or on the bottom channel support assembly, if you choose to not use the optional light stand with your system.*

DIY Hydroponics System Builders Guide

Step #2: Build the Optional Light Stand
(skip this step if you do not want to build the light stand)

A. Build another channel support assembly as you did in Step #1. Attach the two top rails you built in Step # 1D and four 48 inch long pipes as shown.

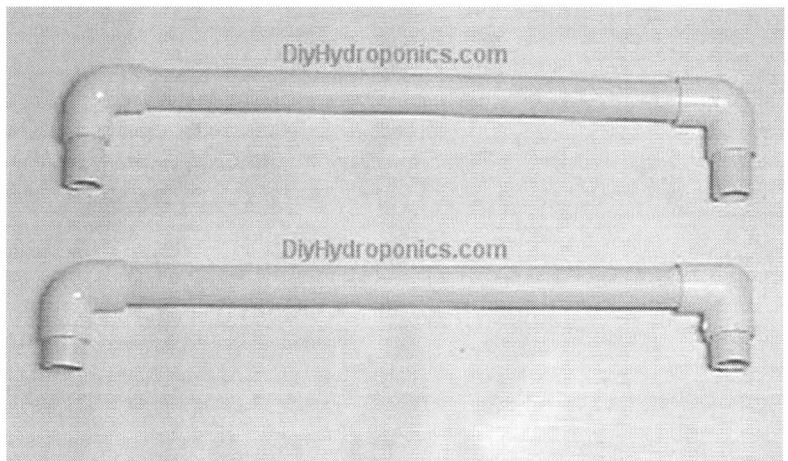

B. Attach the light stand (right) to the bottom support assembly (left).

Bottom Channel Support   *Light stand*

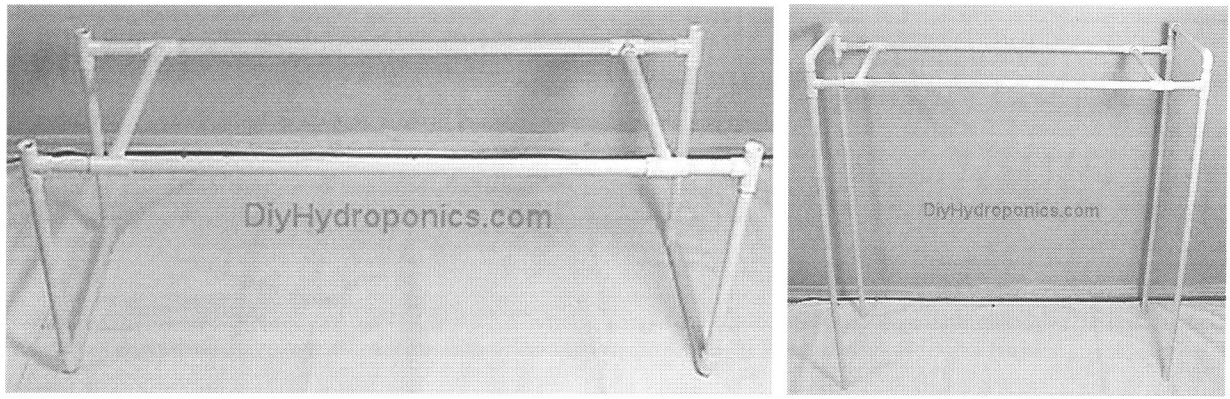

Note: *The height of the channel support assembly and the light stand can be easily adjusted by changing the length of the 16 inch channel support legs or the 48 inch light stand leg pipes*
.

(The assembly of the support stand is now complete!)

Step #3: Install the NFT channel end caps

(Use silicon adhesive or aquarium adhesive to attach and seal the end caps. Let them dry completely).

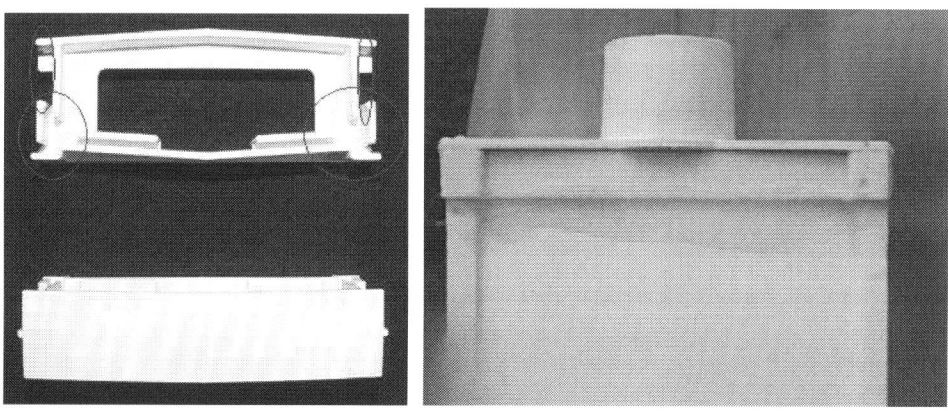

Step #4: Assemble and Install the Drain Assembly using 1 inch PVC Parts.

- 3 – 1 inch PVC elbows
- 1 – 1 inch PVC tee
- 2 – 6 inch long pipes
- 2 – 2 ½ inch long pipes

Use silicon to glue the drain assembly to the drain caps on the NFT channels. You may press together or use silicone glue to connect the rest of the drain assembly (elbows, tee's, etc).

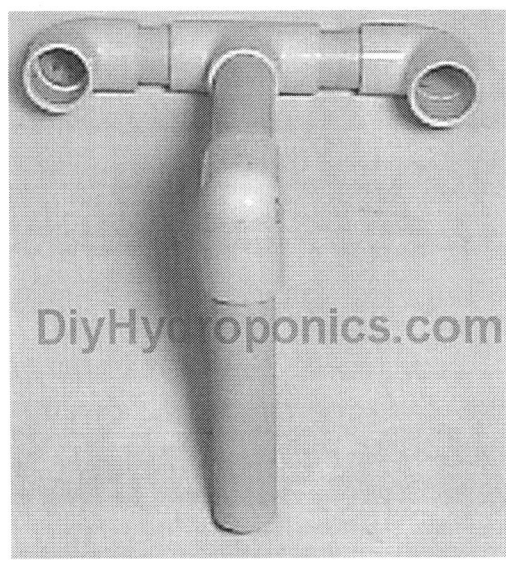

Step #5: How to Build the Clog-free Inlet Manifold

Required Parts:

- 1 – ½ inch male threaded to ½ inch barb adapter
- 2 – ½ inch PVC caps
- 2 – ³/₈ inch threaded barbs
- 2 – 5 ½ inch PVC pipes
- 1 – 64 inch long piece of ½ inch ID flexible tubing
- 1 – ½ inch elbow
- PVC pipe glue or silicone
- Teflon tape

Required Tools: Power drill with 1 small pilot bit, 1 $^5/_{16}$ inch bit, a $^3/_8$ inch tap, tape measure, PVC cutter or hand saw.

A. Take the two 5 ½ x ½ inch PVC pipes and drill a $^5/_{16}$ inch hole, 2 inches from the end of each pipe. Use a small pilot bit to start the hole. Tap the $^5/_{16}$ inch holes with a $^3/_8$ inch tap. Put some Teflon tape on the barb threads and screw them into the tapped holes in the pipes.

B. Glue the two 5 ½ x ½ inch PVC pipes into the ½ inch PVC threaded tee.

C. Glue one ½ inch PVC cap onto the end of each 5 ½ inch long PVC pipe.

D. Use Teflon on the threads and screw the ½ inch adapter into the threaded end of the ½ inch tee.

Note: *If you plan to glue the 5 ½" PVC pipes into the tee. Make sure the barbs are facing straight down when the Tee is horizontal and pointing towards the drain.*

Note: *Just press and then pond tight the PVC parts together. In most cases gluing is optional,*

Note: *You will need to drill holes in the NFT covers to set the inlet manifold into. Another option is to glue the manifold to the channel cover. I use a small piece of $^3/_8$ inch tubing on the barb on the underside of the cover to hold the fill manifold onto the cover.*

(Tools and parts required to build the clog free fill manifold)

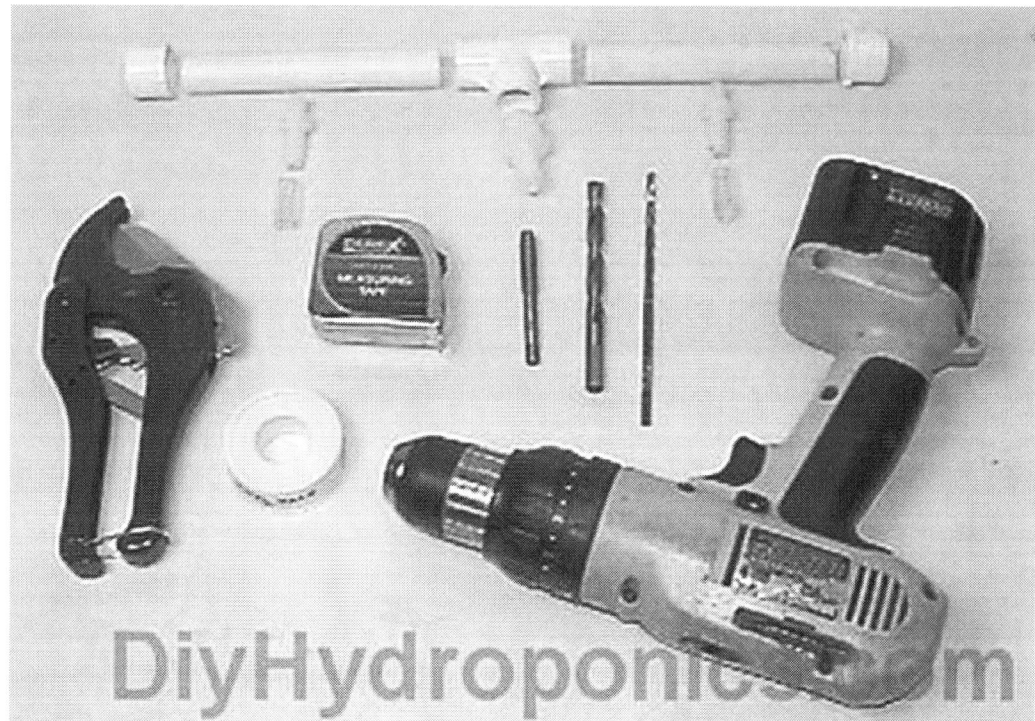

DIY Hydroponics System Builders Guide

Pictures of completed fill manifold.

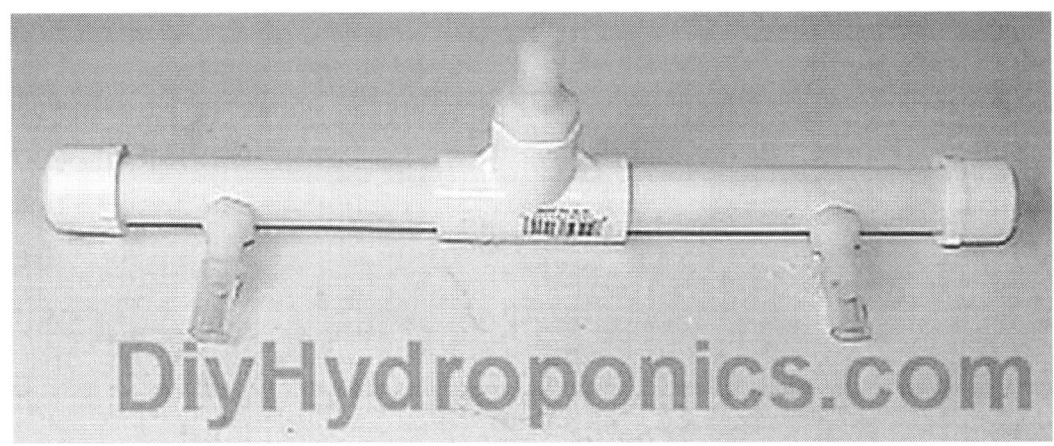

Step #6: Install the Pump into the Reservoir.

Place the pump in the reservoir. You can use any plastic container for a reservoir, such as a bucket, storage container, or plastic ice chest. *DO NOT USE ANY METAL CONTAINERS*. Connect the pump to the inlet manifold with the ½ inch ID flexible tubing. If necessary, use elbows to route the tubing without creating any kinks or sharp bends.

Note: *Do not plug the pump in, until you have water in the reservoir. Running the pump dry may cause damage to the pump.*

Congratulations!

You have completed building the two channel NFT System!
(Continue to the next page for the 4 channel 24 plant upgrade)

Assembling the 24 Plant Upgrade

The 24-plant support stand is exactly the same as the NFT 12. The only exception being that the stand is built wider in order to accommodate four NFT channels. Simply replace the six 16 inch long PVC support pipes with six 30 inch PVC pipes. You will also need the following parts too complete the 24-plant upgrade.

Required Parts:

- 8 – ¾ inch PVC pipes 30 inches long
- 2 – 48 inch NFT channels complete with end caps and cover
- 1 – additional complete inlet manifold (see step 3 – NFT 12 plant instructions)
- 1 – ½ inch tee (used to connect the two inlet manifolds together)
- 2 – 1 inch PVC pipes cut 6 ¼ inch long pieces (for the drain)
- 2 – 1 inch PVC tees (for the drain)
- 2 – 12 inch long pieces of flexible ½ inch ID tubing

DIY Hydroponics System Builders Guide

Step #1: Top and Bottom Stand Adjustment.

Replace the eight 16 inch pipes used with the 12- plant system with eight 30 inch PVC pipes.

Step #2: Assemble the drain as shown.

Use silicon to glue the drain to the NFT channels.

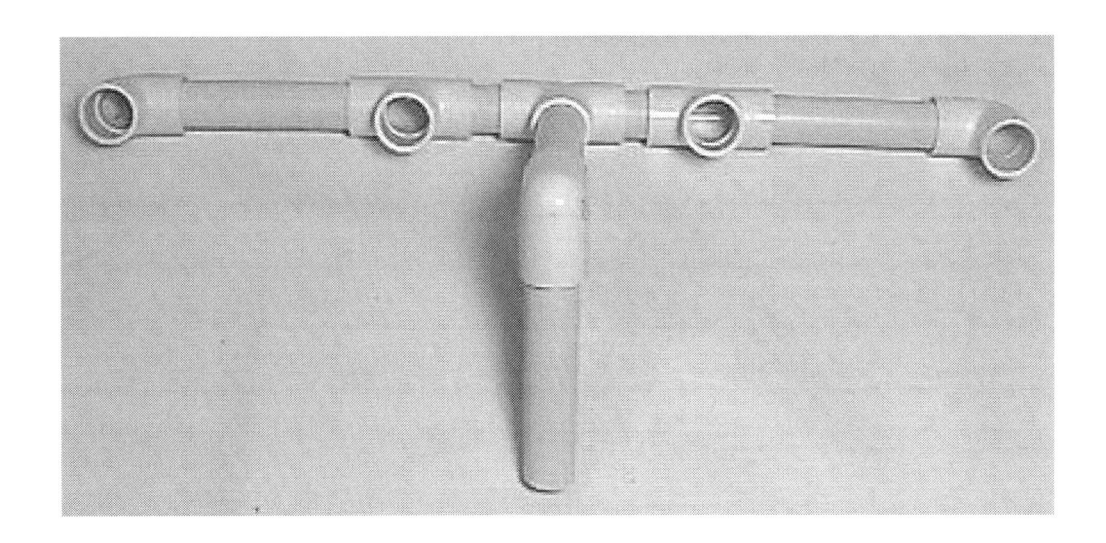

Step #3: Build a second drain manifold

The NFT 24-plant upgrade requires a second inlet manifold to accommodate the two additional channels. Build an additional fill manifold (see step #4), assemble the manifold, and connect the two inlet manifolds together using a ½ inch tee and two 12 inch long pieces of flexible ½ inch ID tubing.

Note: *Alternative NFT fill manifold designs:*

There are other ways to build a fill manifold for your system.

Option #1 – Build the clog-free manifold as instructed above. This is the best way for small systems, but it is also the most work.

Option #2 – This is the easiest method. Run standard ½ inch poly irrigation tubing from the pump to the head of the NFT channels. The poly tubing is rolled over or caped at the end. Punch holes and connect two ¼ inch drip lines into the poly tubing for each NFT Channel. You can use tees and elbows to get the shape you want.

Option #3 – Build the manifold used for the *Bato Bucket System* described earlier in this manual.

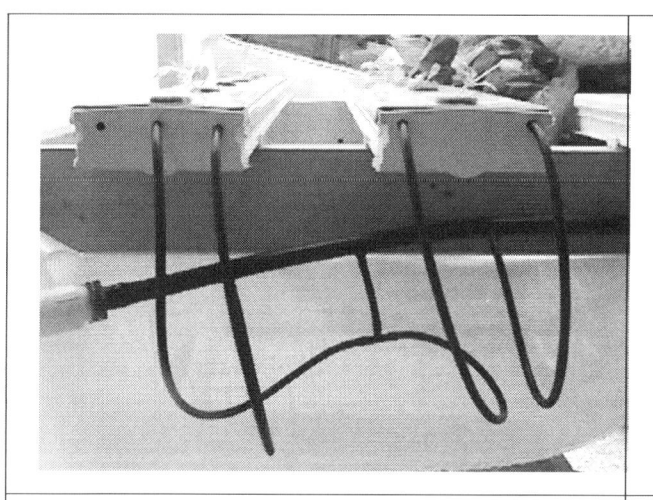

Home built system using poly tubing from pump and ¼ inch drip lines to the channels.

Commercial system using PVC and ¼ inch drip lines. This is the method used by crop king and American Hydroponics for their commercial systems.

Note: Alternate Drain Systems: The channels ends are sometimes left open and a gutter or trough is to catch the nutrient from the channels and route it back to the reservoir tank.

Note: DIY Alternate NFT channels can be built from rain gutters, down spouts, PVC pipes and fence posts. Many builders have been successful using PVC rain gutter down spouts as NFT channels. They are a little smaller than the commercial channels, but work well for short-term plants such as salad greens, herbs, and flowers. Cut the downspouts to the desired length and drill 1 ½ inch holes starting 4 inches from the inlet side then spacing 8 inches apart on center. You can leave the channels open on the ends or make some caps. I suggest you cut some of the downspout material and silicon it into the inlet side of the channel, making a cap. This will prevent light from entering the channel and keep water from splashing out. You can leave the drain ends open and build a trough out of a piece of open gutter to catch the nutrient and direct it back to the reservoir. For a larger NFT channel you can use rain gutters. Get the U or D style gutters. Solid caps are available for these gutters. You will have to find something solid to cover the gutter with. I made mine out of some vinyl house siding that I cut to fit over some gutter leaf covers.

DIY Hydroponics System Builders Guide

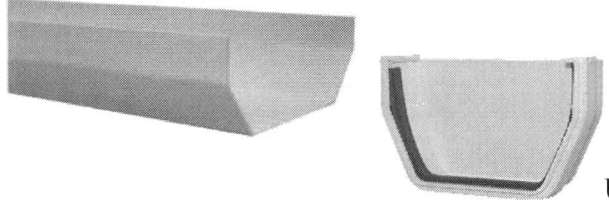

U –style Raingo gutters from Lowes

Down spouts with ends open

PVC pipe channels

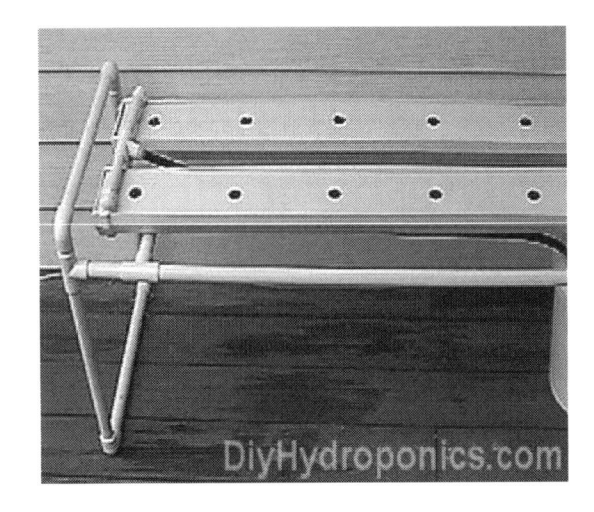

My home made rain gutter system

Closed system using poly irrigation tubing.

How to Build NFT Channels from U-style Rain Gutters

I built these NFT channels from parts I purchased at Lowe's. They ended up costing a little less than the Crop King channels. They were a lot of work to build, however they do work well, and all the parts were found locally at Lowes building supply.

Note: The gutter comes in 10 foot long sections. You can make one 10 foot channel or cut it to whatever size you want. I cut mine to 4 feet and made two NFT channels.

Required Materials for each NFT Channel:

- 1 – plastic rain gutter
- 2 – rain gutter end caps
- 1 – rain gutter leaf guard (fits inside the gutter)
- 1 – solid rain gutter cover (used to cover the one with holes)
- 2 – 1 inch threaded PVC couplers (one with male and one female thread)
- 1 – 1 ¼ inch ID – lavatory pop-up drain gasket (fits over the male coupler)
- 1 – Electric drill with a 1 ¼ inch and 1 inch bits
- Hacksaw, Box knife, tape measure, marker and silicon glue

Step #1: Use a hacksaw to cut the rain gutter. Use a scissors or a box knife to cut the covers. You can use any materials you can find to make a cover. I used two different materials to make my covers and glued them together to make one solid cover.

Step #2: Drill a 1 ¼ inch hole inside one end of the gutter for the drain. Be sure you drill far enough from the end of the gutter to get the end cap on.

Step #3: Use a hacksaw to cut the coupler with the male thread so that as little as possible sticks up inside the gutter. Put the male threaded coupler into the drain hole from inside the gutter. You can use silicon around the threads or a rubber washer to help seal it. Thread on the female threaded coupler and tighten.

Note: See the first picture with the pen pointing to the place to cut the coupler.

Step #4: Put the end caps on the gutters. You may use silicon to make a watertight seal. I suggest test fitting everything first.

Step# 5: Fit the covers into the gutter. Trim as necessary to make a good fit. Glue as required.

Step# 6: Use the 1 inch drill bit to drill the plant sites into the top of the covers. Normal spacing is 8 inches between plant sites, but you can space however you would like.

DIY Hydroponics System Builders Guide

Pictures of DIY NFT channels created from rain gutters

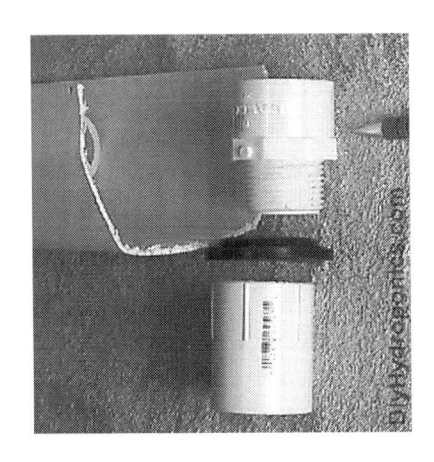

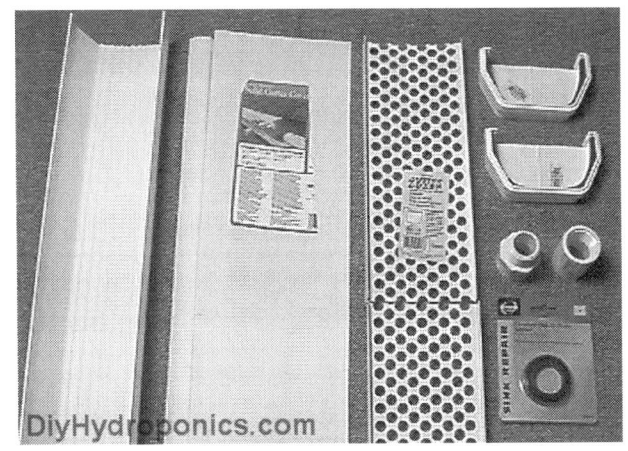

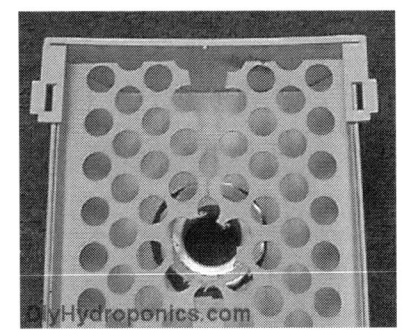

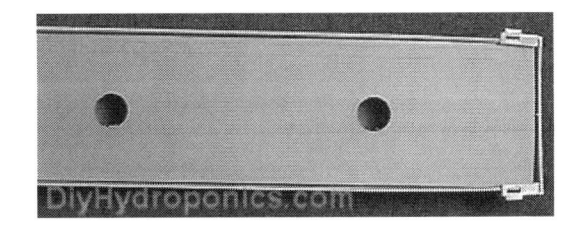

DiyHydroponics.com

Tips for Testing, Adjusting, and Increasing Performance of your NFT System

Check for leaks - Put enough water in your reservoir to cover the pump and plug it in. Make sure all the channels fill and drain without any leaks. If anything leaks, press the pipes more tightly together or use silicon to seal.

Slope the channels - In order to reduce the chances of water pooling inside the NFT channel, all channels should have a slope of 1:30 to 1:40 raise the fill end of the stand or the channels up to 1 inch higher than the drain end. A thin film of water should flow quickly through each channel. Adjust the channel slope and use the flow control valve on the pump until you get a good even flow. One method used to create a slope in the channels, is too shorten the downhill leg pipes. Regardless of the channel length, NFT flow should be 1 liter per minute, with a maximum of 2 liters per minute, which is about 34 ounces.

Note: *You can also, use sloping to adjust the depth of the nutrient in the channel. Raise the drain side of the channel and the depth of nutrient increases. Temporarily increasing the nutrient depth is useful when starting new plants and their roots are not reaching the bottoms of the channels. After roots are better established, adjust the slop again so only a thin layer of nutrient is flowing.*

Nutrient temperature - Ideally, a nutrient temperature of 18 to 22° C (65-72° F) should be maintained for optimum growth, although this may change depending upon the crop and location of the system. Shield your reservoir from the sun or use insulation to keep the nutrient cool. If your nutrient is too cold, insulate the reservoir tank, put a heating pad under the trays, or use a fish tank heater to warm the nutrient.

Ventilation - Plants like air moving all around them. Add fans to help circulate the air around the plants.

Oxygen – Make sure the water draining into the reservoir splashes as it enters the reservoir. This action helps introduce oxygen into the nutrient tank. Another method of increasing oxygen in the reservoir is to Use a small aquarium air pump and air stone to pump air into the reservoir.

Cleaning your system - Between feedings, flush the systems with clean water. This will help remove excess minerals and algae from the system. Between plantings, remove the channel covers and clean all debris from the system. Flush everything with water, clean with a 10% bleach solution, and wipe dry.

DIY Hydroponics System Builders Guide

Pictures of my 2 Channel NFT System

Chapter 4: MPT Tray Systems for Wheat Grass and MicroGreens
(Optional covers available for any system)

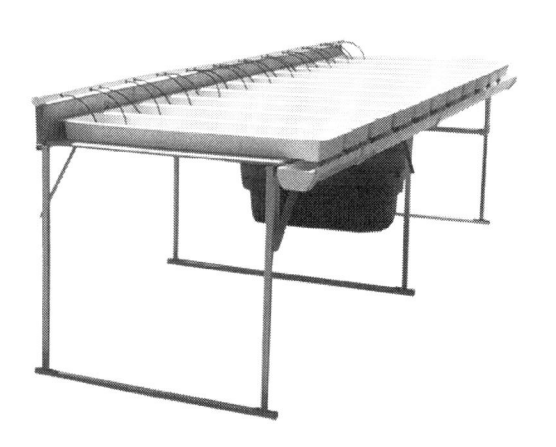

Introduction:

This system is based around the American Hydroponics white MPT propagation tray. The trays cost $25.00 to $35.00 each and can be purchased directly from American Hydroponics. You can build a PVC stand for the trays or lay them out on any flat surface or table. The American Hydroponics propagation systems use a platform stand build out of 1 inch galvanized square tube and a plywood top. The MPT trays have two knockouts in one end. Typically, one 1 inch hole is drilled in one of the knockouts and a drain fitting is installed. The drain feeds into a PVC pipe or open trough (rain gutter), whereby the nutrient is routed back to the reservoir. For the fill manifold, AmHydro uses a ½ inch PVC pipe drilled for ³/₈ inch grommets and ¼ inch drip lines (same as the Bato Bucket system described in this manual.) Optionally, as with the single tray system in this manual, the second hole can be drilled for a custom fill manifold or Ebb & Flow fittings.

How it works:

The systems operate much like a NFT system except rather than using a flat bottom tray and a very thin film of water. These trays have a ridged bottom causing the water to trickle through the tray, like a small stream running over a rocky surface. This type of bottom feed is ideal for wheatgrass, and microgreens because it allows the top of the plants to remain dry, thereby reducing the risk of mold growth.

DIY Hydroponics System Builders Guide

The ultimate in flexibility:

Because of the depth and width of the trays they are suitable for almost any plant. Covers can be made and drilled for net pots, or pots can be set directly in the trays. Trays can also be easily converted from trickle feed to ebb & flow, top feed or aeroponic operations.

Example #1 Single Tray System

Parts List:

- American Hydroponics white MPT Tray
- 1 – small submersible pump
- 1 – reservoir
- 1 – fill assembly
- 1 – drain assembly
- 1 – PVC stand
- 1 – optional 3 inch net pot top cover and net pots

PVC Stand Parts: (use 1" PVC pipe)

- 2 – 43 ¼ inch rails
- 4 – 10 ½ inch cross members
- 4 – 2 inch PVC pieces (used to connect tees to elbows)
- 2 – 20 inch legs (adjust the 4 leg pipes to the desired stand height)
- 2 – 19 inch legs (these are the lower legs, they are 1 inch shorter to help with draining)
- 4 – tees
- 8 – elbows

Parts for fill assembly:

- 1 – ¾ inch male threaded to ½ inch hose bib adapter
- 1 – ¾ inch rubber washer
- 1 – coupler with female threads on both ends
- 1 – ¾ inch coupler to ¾ inch male threaded
- 1 – ¾ inch to ½ inch female threaded adapter
- 1 – 1/2 inch CPVC coupler to ½ inch male threaded adapter
- 1 – ½ inch CPVC special elbow with pipe on one end and coupler on the other
- 3 – ½ inch CPVC elbows
- 1 – CPVC cap
- 1 – ½ inch CPVC pipe 1 & ½ inch
- 1 – ½ inch CPVC pipe 8 & ³/₈ inch
- 1 – ½ inch CPVC pipe 40 & ¹/₈ inch

Parts for drain assembly:

- 1 – modified ¾ inch male threaded coupler and rubber washer (cut it off as directed)
- 1 – ¾ inch Female threaded coupler

DIY Hydroponics System Builders Guide

- **Step #1**: Assemble the stand – Cut and press the PVC pieces together as shown in the pictures.

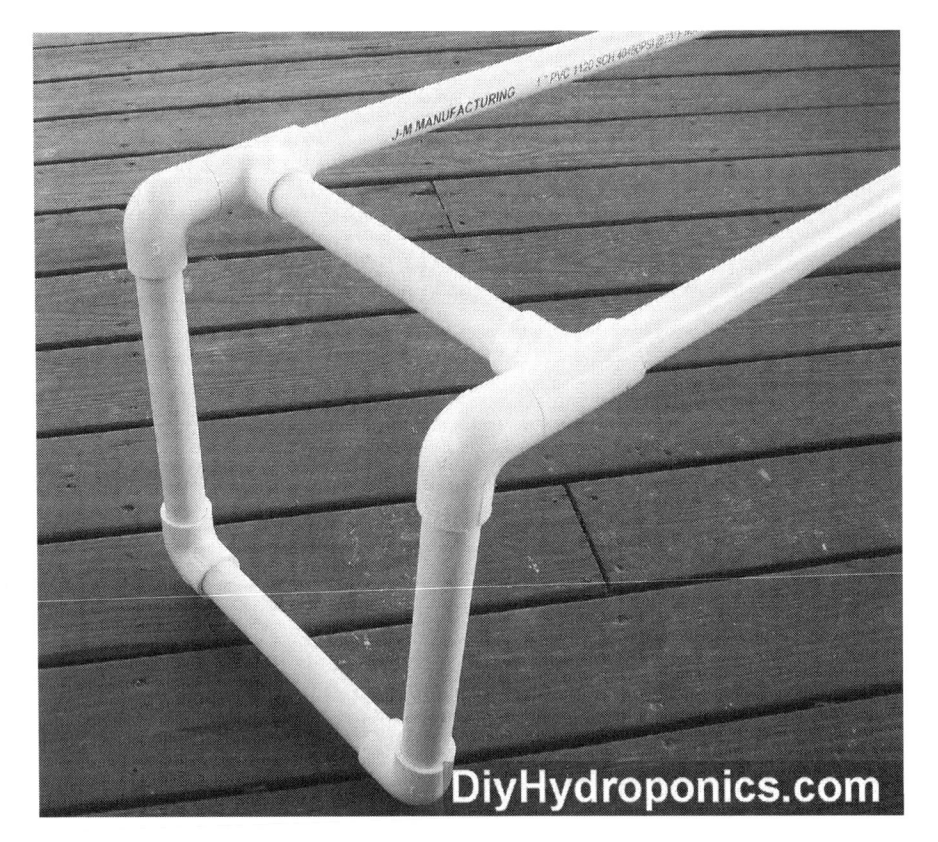

Note: *Do not forget to use the two shorter legs on the drain end of the stand.*

Step #2: Drill a 1inch hole in both of the MPT tray knockouts.
Step #3: Drill 4 ¼ inch holes in the 8 inch CPVC Pipe and assemble the fill line as shown in bottom picture.

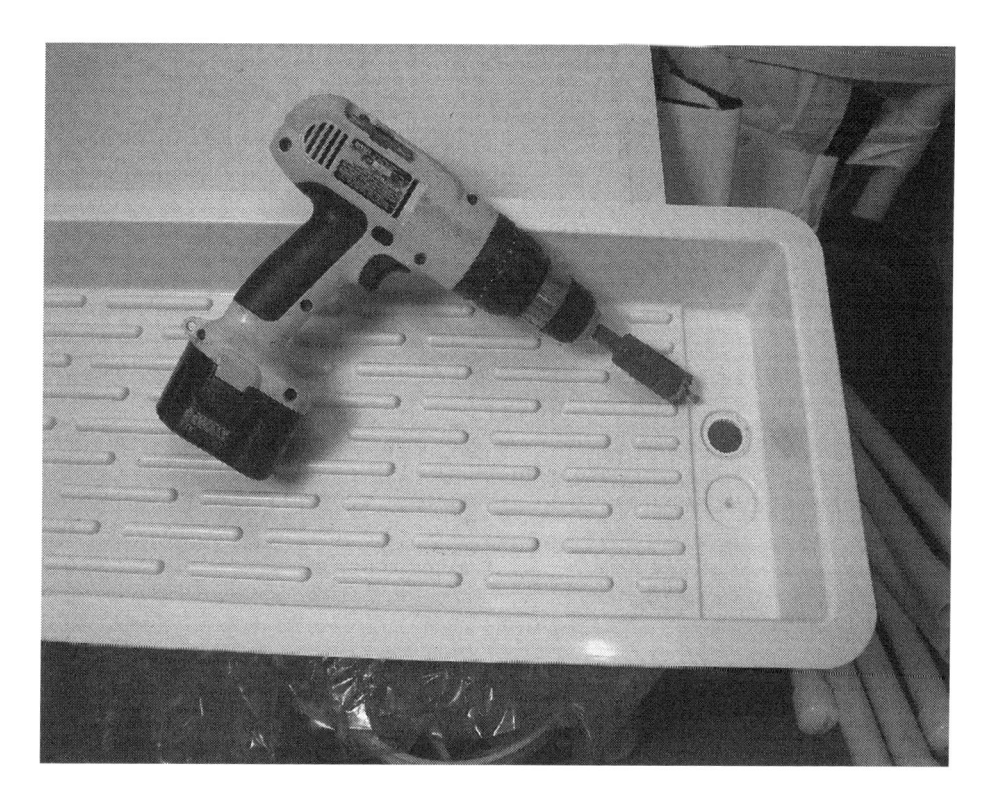

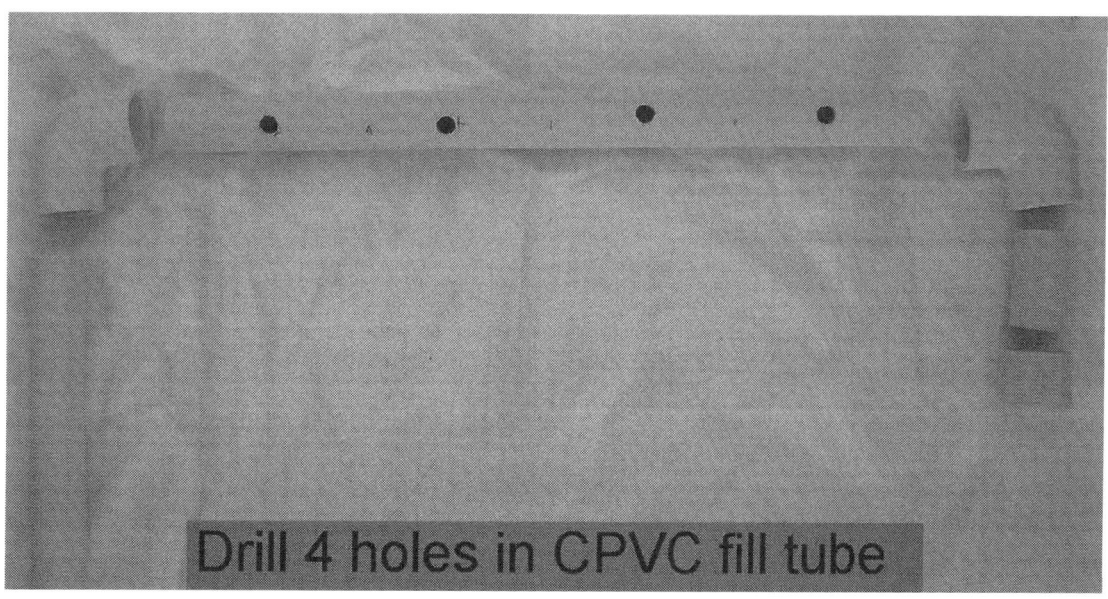

Drill 4 holes in CPVC fill tube

DIY Hydroponics System Builders Guide

Step #3: Drill 4 ¼ inch holes in the 8 inch CPVC Pipe and assemble the fill line as pictured.

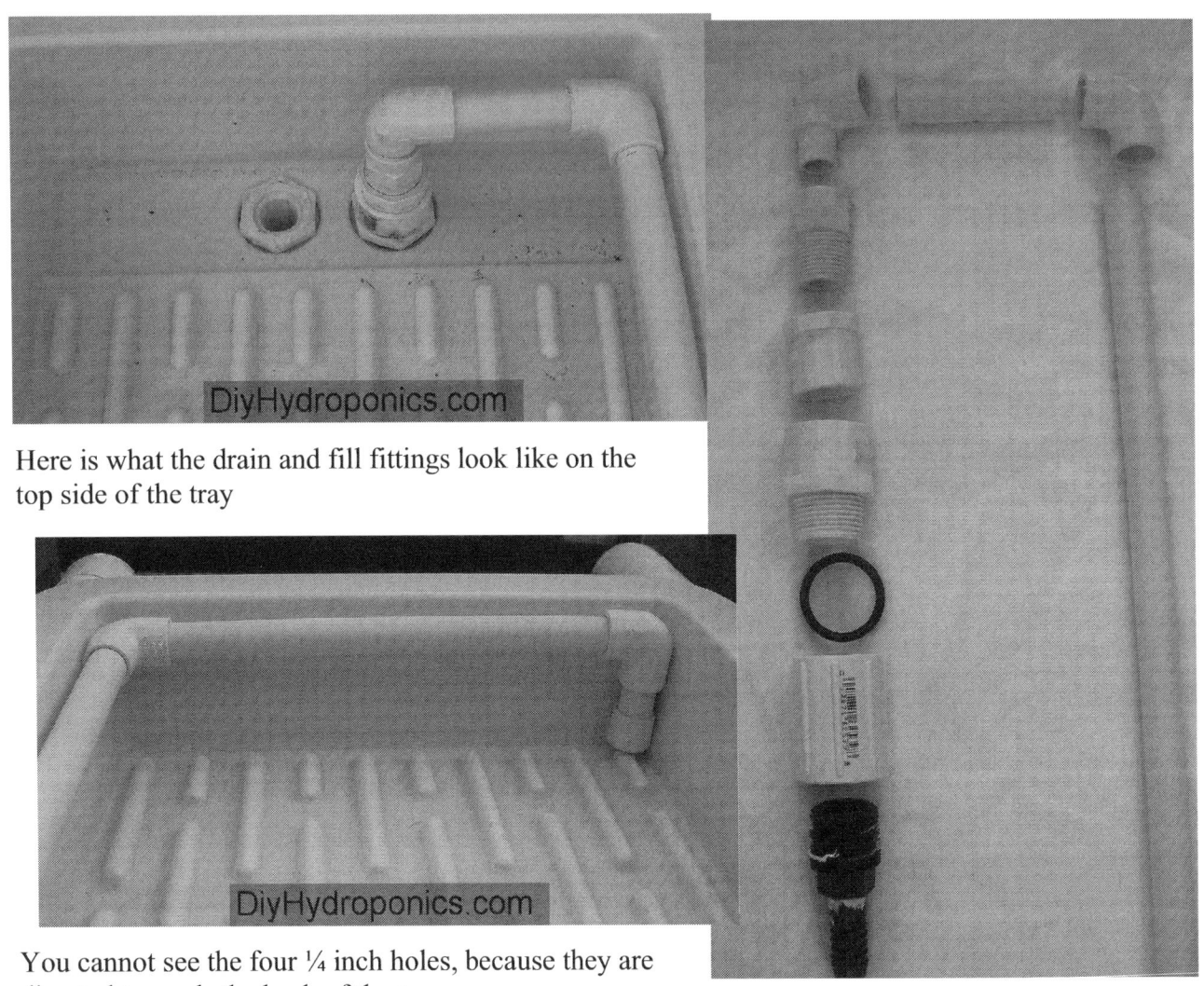

Here is what the drain and fill fittings look like on the top side of the tray

You cannot see the four ¼ inch holes, because they are directed towards the back of the tray

The male threaded coupler and washer, go through the hole in the top of the tray and the female threaded coupler goes underneath the tray.

Step #4: Cut one of the male threaded couplers off with a hack saw as shown

Before cut

After cut

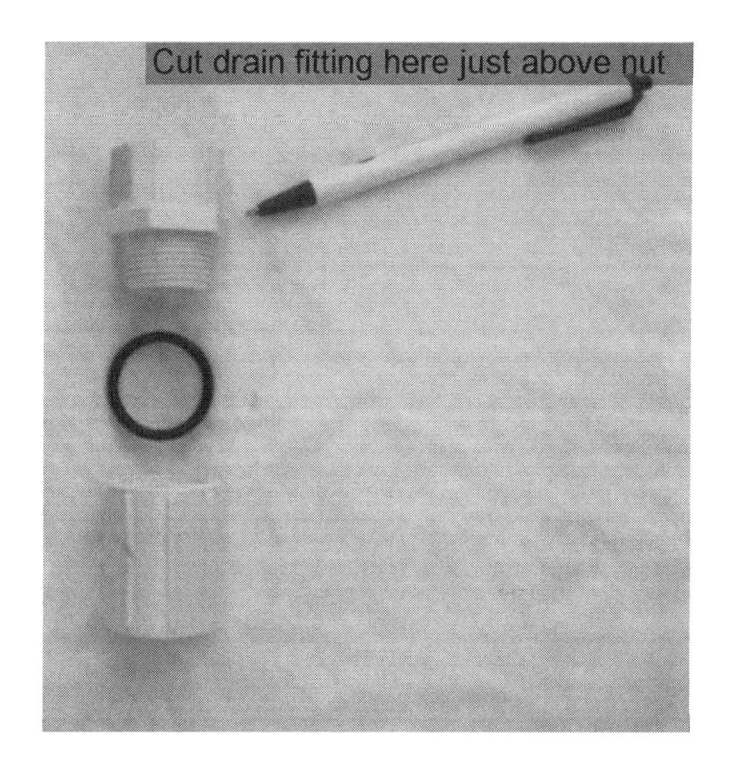

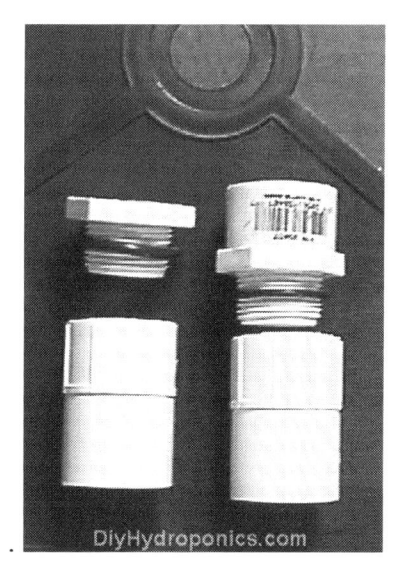

Cut drain fitting here just above nut

cut coupler off here

(The finished cut drain fitting on left and un-cut fill fitting on right)

DIY Hydroponics System Builders Guide

Step #5: Install the fill and drain lines into tray.

Put the rubber washer on the male threaded couplers and push through the top of the tray. Attach the double female threaded couplers underneath the tray and hand tightens. Connect all the other parts together as shown in the pictures. For an improved seal you may use Teflon tape on all the male threads. Because the system runs on low pressure, gluing the pipes is not usually necessary; however, you may need to use pipe glue or silicone sealant if you have a leak.

Step # 6: Put the tray on the stand and connect up to the pump with ½ inch ID flexible tubing. If necessary, extend the tray drain with small piece of ¾ inch PVC pipe.

(Bottom of tray showing the fill and drain connections.)

MPT Tray Cover

American Hydroponics does not currently offer covers for the MPT trays; however, you can build your own DIY covers. Tray covers are used in two different ways. For Micro-Greens and Wheat Grass, a solid cover is used to cover the seeds while sprouting. If you desire to grow other plants, drill holes in the covers to accommodate starter cubes or net pots. DIY covers can be made out of any plastic material or even wood if covered with poly sheeting. All the covers in the pictures were made with water board from Home Depot and drilled for 3 inch net pots. Water board is the material used to cover the walls in bath and shower stalls. The material comes in 4 x 8 sheets and is readily available. Too build the covers, simple cut them out to fit the trays and drill them with a hole saw. The examples in the pictures show a solid cover used for sprouting, a cover with eight 3 inch holes for small plants and a cover with only four 3 inch holes for large plants.

Pictures of MPT Trays and covers

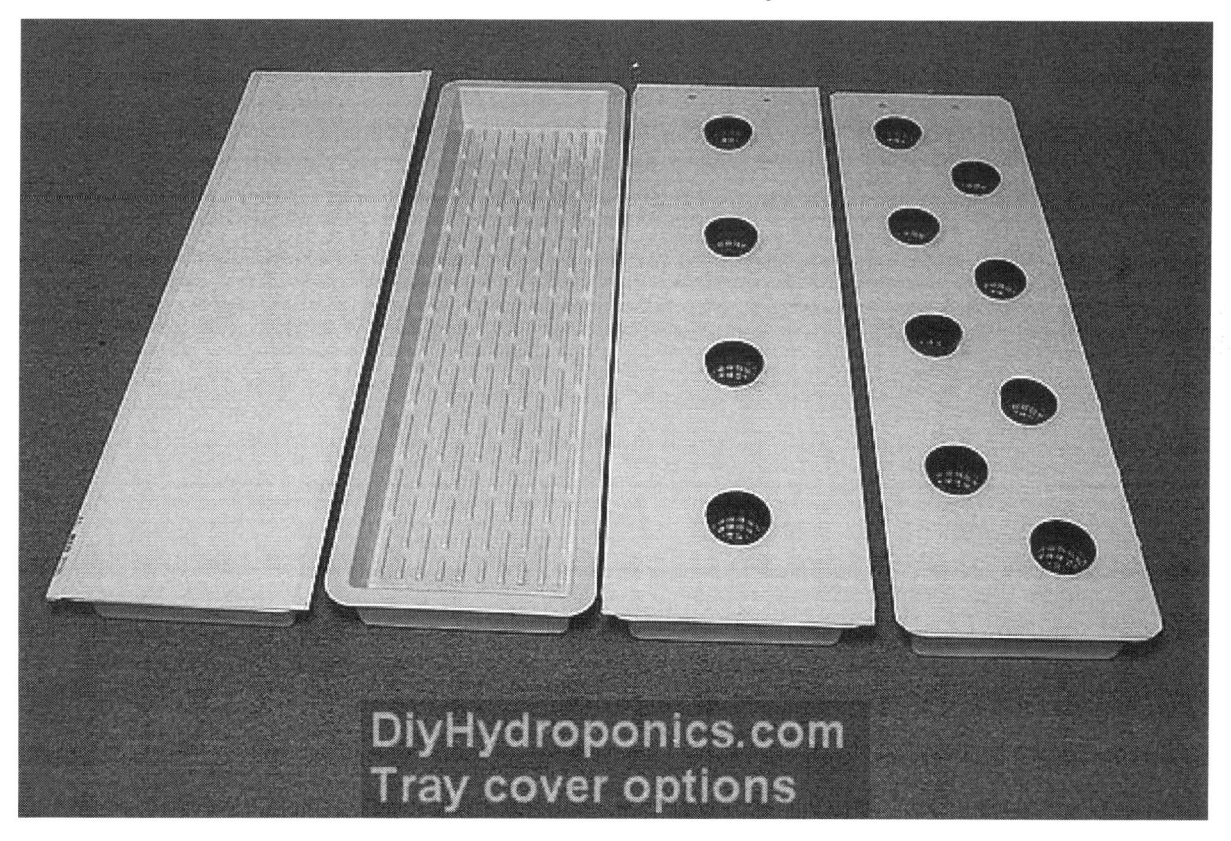

DIY Hydroponics System Builders Guide

Multiple Tray Systems

Building a two tray System:

Pictured here are examples of a two-tray system with a PVC stand. Build the drain and fill manifold for each tray, the same as you did for the single tray system, except use elbows rather than straight couplers on the drain and then tie them together with a tee as shown. For the PVC stand simply widen the one tray stand to accommodate two trays. Use the pictures below, as a guide

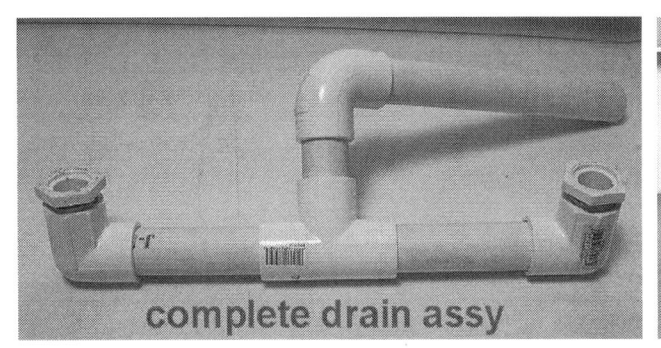

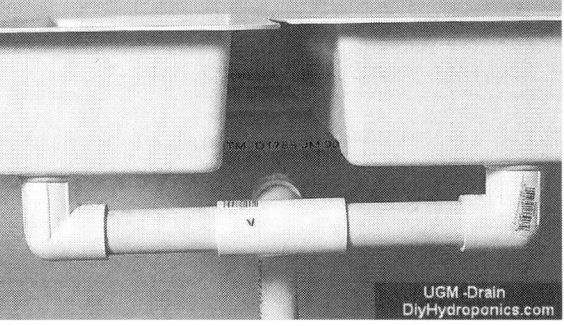

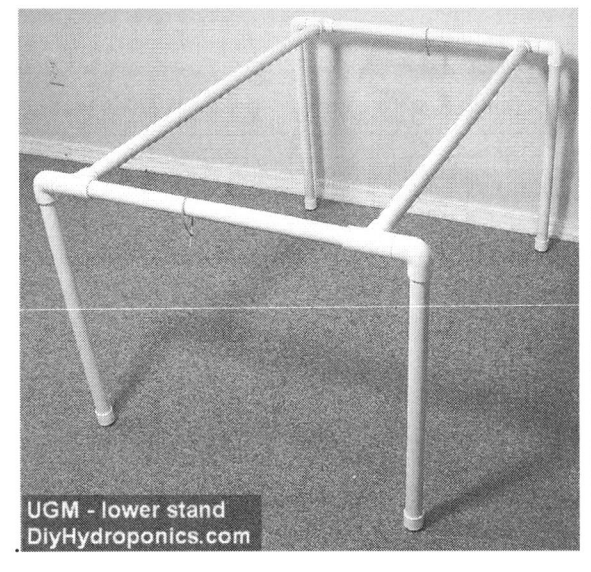

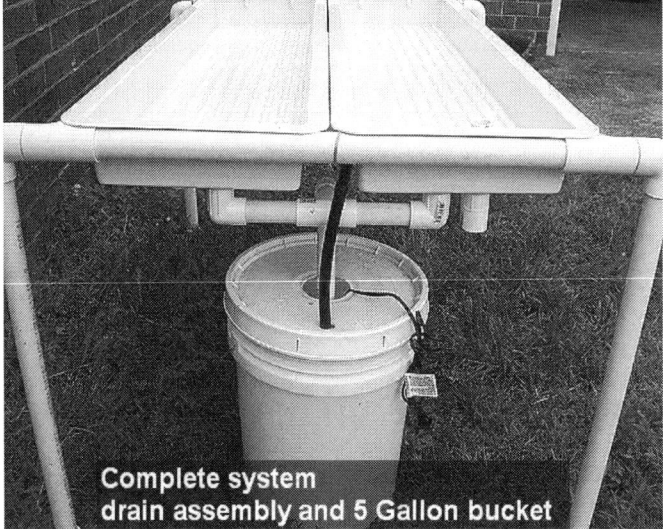

Note: *Remember to make the legs 1 inch shorter on the drain end to set the slope.*

DiyHydroponics.com

Pictures of some MPT Systems

DIY Hydroponics System Builders Guide

DiyHydroponics.com

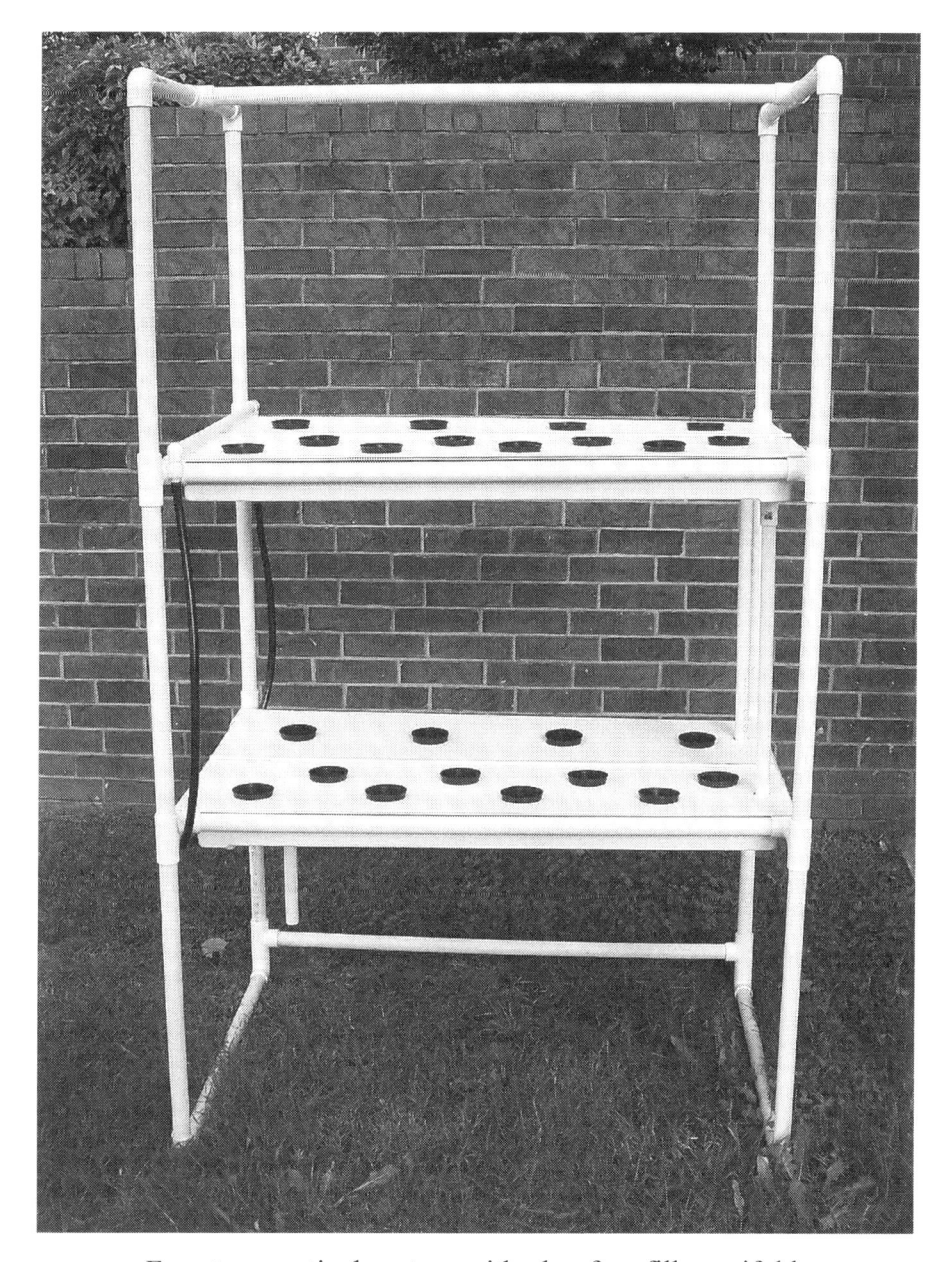

Four tray vertical system with clog free fill manifold.

Note: Instructions for growing Wheatgrass and Micro-greens in this system are included in the *Diy Hydroponics Master Library* through our website **DiyHydroponics.com**

Hydroponic Resources

Diy Hydroponics
P.O Box 752 Berryville AR. 72616
(870) 619-4141
Web Address: www.DiyHydroponics.com

Crop King Inc. – (NFT Channels)
134 West Drive Lodi, Ohio 44254
Phone: (330) 302-4203 , Toll free (800)321-5656

American Hydroponics (NFT Channels and MPT Trays)
286 South G street, Arcata CA. 95521
(800) 458-6543 or (707) 822-5777.

General Hydroponics
P.O. Box 1576, Sebastopol, CA 95473
(1-800-374-9376) or 1-707-824-9376

Midwest Hydroponics
3440 Beltline Blvd. Minneapolis, MN 55416
952-925-9835, 888-449-2739

Marine Depot – (Pumps)
14271 Corporate Drive, Garden Grove, CA 92843
Phone:1-800-566-3474, 1-714-385-0080

Best Grow Lights
2028 Fort Perry Road
Box Springs, GA 31801
Web Address: www.bestgrowlights.com
Email: sales@bestgrowlights.com
Phone: Toll Free 800-337-1060

Johnny's Selected Seeds
955 Benton Avenue, Winslow, Maine
04901 Phone: Toll Free: 1-877-Johnnys (1-877-564-6697)

The Growing Edge Magazine
P.O. Box 1027, Corvallis, OR USA 97339-1027
USA: (800) 888-6785,

Glossary of Terms

Aeroponics: a variation of hydroponics that involves the misting of plant roots with nutrient solution.

Anther: part at the top of the male flower that produces the pollen.

Aquaponics: the integration of aquaculture (the raising of marine animals, such as fish) with hydroponics; the waste products from the fish are treated and then used to fertilize hydroponically growing plants.

Bato Buckets: or "dutch pots" are a form of drip system that is enclosed except for the top of the growing surface. The nutrient is never exposed to sunlight, therefore no algae will grow. The outlet system prevents roots from plugging the outlet line. It has a reservoir in case of pump failure or can be operated with a timer.

Bolting: for a plant to prematurely begin the development of a flowering stalk and, subsequently, seed.

Capillary action: when the surface of a liquid is in contact with a solid, the liquid is elevated or depressed depending upon the relative attraction of the molecules of the liquid for each other or for those of the solid. This is similar to how plants seemingly defy gravity when they transport liquid from the roots upward through the plant.

Chlorophyll: the green material in plants that is created in the presence of light and is instrumental in photosynthesis.

Closed system: A hydroponic system, like nutrient film technique (NFT) systems, that recalculates the nutrient solution.

Conductivity: the scale, described as electrical conductivity (EC) or conductivity factor (CF), that is used to measure the strength of nutrient solution.

Germination: the activation of a seed causing it to start to grow; also the production of a pollen tube by a pollen grain

Growing medium: materials that are sometimes used in hydroponic growing to support the plant's roots and, sometimes, to hold nutrient.

Macronutrients: the major minerals that are used by plants in large amounts, consisting of nitrogen (N), phosphorus (P), potassium (K), sulfur (S), calcium (Ca), and magnesium (Mg).

Micro-greens: Seedlings harvested when the first true leaves appear (just after the cotyledon or seed leaf stage).Micro-greens: Seedlings harvested when the first true leaves appear (just after the cotyledon or seed leaf stage).

Micronutrients: the minor minerals that are used by plants in small amounts, consisting of boron (B), copper (Cu), cobalt (Co), iron (Fe), manganese (Mn), molybdenum (Mo), and zinc (Zn).

Mineral deficiency: when a plant is not receiving a required nutrient--at all or in an insufficient amount--a disorder will result.

MPT System: Multiple Tray System

NFT: or Nutrient film technique, whereby a very shallow stream of water containing all the dissolved nutrients required for plant growth is recirculated past the bare roots of plants in a watertight thick root mat, which develops in the bottom of the channel, has an upper surface that, although moist, is in the air.

Nutrient solution: minerals dissolved in water that are used to feed hydroponically grown plants.

Parts per million (ppm): a ratio figure that represents the amount of one substance that is in one million parts of another substance; commonly used to describe the relative concentrations of nutrient solutions.

pH: a measurement of a nutrient solution's relative concentration of positive hydrogen ions: a pH of 7 is considered neutral; below 7 is called acidic; above 7 is called alkaline.

Photosynthesis: the formation of carbohydrates from carbon dioxide (CO_2) and a source of hydrogen (H)--such as water--in chlorophyll-containing cells exposed to light involving a photochemical release of oxygen through the decomposition of water.

Wheatgrass: A food prepared from the cotyledons of the common wheat plant, Triticum aestivum. It is sold either as a juice or powder concentrate. It provides chlorophyll, amino acids, minerals, vitamins, and enzymes. Claims about the health benefits of wheatgrass range from providing supplemental nutrition to having unique curative properties.

Wick: woven fiber used in some hydroponic systems to draw nutrient to a plant's roots through capillary action.

DIY Hyroponics Master Library!
(DIY Hydroponics 101)
10 Volume Set of Hydroponic Gardening eBooks

Getting Started With Hydroponics 123	The Bible of Hydroponic Gardening. Includes 450 pages, over 100 color pictures, charts, references and plans.
The DAMA'S Hydroponic Guide	Covers every aspect of Hydroponic Gardening. Fully illustrated with over 80 full color pictures. Includes DFT and Hanging Bag Systems.
Grow With The Flow	47 page eBook includes basics, youth projects and instructions including horizontal and vertical hydroponic systems.
How To Grow Hydroponics	Read this book first! An excellent beginner's book on hydroponic gardening includes 58 well illustrated pages.
Hydroponics Secrets Revealed	This report is filled with special tips and tricks to help you save money and increase the harvest of your hydroponic system.
Barrel-ponics Aquaponic System Plans (Free from Travis W. Hughey)	Barrel-ponics is a unique way, to inexpensively build an aquaponics system using surplus plastic barrels. Much thanks to Travis for his great work.
DIY Hydroponic System Builders Guide	Plans for building your own hydroponic systems. Plans included for several variation of systems. Including: Top Feed, Ebb & Flow, NFT and more.
Build Your Own Hobby Greenhouses	Build your own DIY greenhouses. Includes plans for building structures made of wood, PVC pipe and steel.
Systems Builders Guide	Systems Builders Guide in full color digital form.
Greenhouse Builders Guide	How to build your own greenhouses from PVC, metal or wood.

DIY Hydroponic Master Library

Everything you need to know about hydroponic gardening.

Download the *DIY Hydroponics Master Library* and get all 10 volumes of the Hydroponic eBooks from our website or order it on a CD.

Full 10 volume set!

Download only $9.99 or get the CD for only $14.99

(Free shipping)

DiyHydroponics.com

Our guarantee: If for any reason you are not satisfied with your purchase of **The DIY Hydroponic Library**, you may return it within 10 days of purchase for a full refund.

Printed in Poland
by Amazon Fulfillment
Poland Sp. z o.o., Wrocław